A POCKET GUIDE TO

PIGEON
WATCHING

Getting to Know the World's
Most Misunderstood Bird

A POCKET GUIDE TO
PIGEON
WATCHING

Getting to Know the World's
Most Misunderstood Bird

ROSEMARY MOSCO

Workman Publishing
NEW YORK

Library of Congress Cataloging-in-Publication Data is available.

ISBN 978-1-5235-1134-1

Cover illustration by Rosemary Mosco
Design and cover by Sarah Smith

Workman books are available at special discounts when purchased in bulk for premiums and sales promotions as well as for fundraising or educational use. Special editions or book excerpts can also be created to specification. For details, contact the Special Sales Director at specialmarkets@workman.com.

Workman Publishing Co., Inc.
225 Varick Street
New York, NY 10014-4381

workman.com

WORKMAN is a registered trademark of Workman Publishing Co., Inc.

Printed in China on paper from responsible sources
First printing August 2021

10 9 8 7 6 5 4 3 2

To my dad, Vincent Mosco, who grew up in a
Manhattan tenement and only knew three kinds
of birds: the gray ones, the little brown ones,
and seagulls. Dad, thanks for helping me see the
connections that make the world work.
Here are some more connections for you.

CONTENTS

INTRODUCTION

WHY WATCH PIGEONS? 1

PART 1

BASIC PIGEONOLOGY
Why Pigeons Are Dinosaurs,
Doves, and Puppies 9

PART 2

THE PASSION AND THE POOP
A History of Pigeons and People 27

PART 3

PIGEONATOMY
From Beak to Cloaca 61

PART 4

DOMESTIC PIGEON BREEDS
The Fanciest Flock 87

PART 5

FERAL PLUMAGES AND PATTERNS
Spot Them All.. **103**

PART 6

DECODING PIGEON BEHAVIOR
Why Is That Pigeon Doing That Thing? **125**

PART 7

PIGEON TROUBLESHOOTING
How to Stay Healthy and Help Pigeons **185**

EXTRA CREDIT
Other Birds Worth Watching.......................**201**

CONCLUSION **223**
FURTHER READING.......................................**224**
SELECTED REFERENCES...............................**226**
ACKNOWLEDGMENTS....................................**231**
ABOUT THE AUTHOR....................................**232**

WHY WATCH PIGEONS?

I will show you my pigeons!
Which is the greatest treat, in my opinion,
which can be offered to [a] human being.

—CHARLES DARWIN

How do you feel about pigeons?

Maybe you hate them. Tons of people do. Perhaps you loathe their dusty-looking feathers, or the way they swarm the sidewalks, or the fact that they're allowed to poop anywhere they want, but YOU always have to find a bathroom.

Or maybe you're just apathetic about pigeons. That's a common sentiment, too. For most of us, pigeons are mundane fixtures of life; they're mere flickers of movement in the background. Pigeons aren't flashy or vivid—they're gray, white, or red-brown, the colors of metal, concrete, and dirt. They're not very loud. They can be pests, but they don't sting or bite. Nobody shows up on the nightly news with dramatic gashes from a pigeon attack. Pigeons are just sort of *there*.

But these birds are an important part of the background. You'll find them almost everywhere, on every continent but Antarctica, from the northern tip of Norway to the southern tip of Chile and on lonely islands out in the middle of the ocean. They coo, peck, and nest in most of the world's towns and cities. In fact, they're such a critical part of the metropolitan scenery that movie directors go out of their way to include them in

THERE'S A PIGEON MOVIE DATABASE

Want to know more about pigeons in movies? The Pigeon Movie Database (PMDb) is a truly astonishing project that tracks pigeons' appearances in films and discusses their symbolism. It also pays tribute to film characters that are friendly to pigeons, including the birdseed seller from *Mary Poppins* and Roy Batty from *Blade Runner.* Visit it at pigeonmoviedatabase.com.

urban shots. For the climactic scene of the movie *Home Alone 2: Lost in New York*, animal handlers carefully trained 500 pigeons to sit, stay, and fly to hidden cages outside the camera's view. Only about 200 birds were present in any given shot, and handlers regularly rotated out the birds so that Hollywood's rigorous filming schedule wouldn't tire them.

How did pigeons become so ubiquitous that movie directors would go to this much trouble? The answer will shock you. Until recently, pigeons weren't just extras in the movies of our lives. They were the *stars*. People all over the world kept them as pets, held pigeon beauty contests, ate them in gourmet dishes, and pitted them against each other in high-stakes races. (In many places, these traditions persist; in others, they're on the rise. There are probably pigeon keepers near you.)

Pigeons are superstars.

Throughout much of the history of warfare, soldiers strapped canisters with important messages to the legs, bellies, or backs of pigeons. When the birds braved artillery fire and gas to successfully deliver their intel, people rewarded them with prestigious medals. Wherever pigeon keepers traveled, they carted their birds with them. Some pigeons flew the coop and went feral; that's why you can find them in places they didn't originally inhabit, like North and South America and Australia. Pigeons are everywhere, and people are to blame.

Some of our most notable historical figures were pigeon-obsessed. The Mughal emperor Akbar treasured his birds and used them to impress his guests. Who needs a glass of fine wine when you can feast your eyes on a pigeon? The great

A PIGEON BY ANY OTHER NAME

Here are a few non-English names for the pigeon:

Afrikaans: *Tuinduif*

Arabic: حمامة صخري

Chinese: 野鴿

Dutch: *Rotsduif*

French: *Pigeon biset*

German: *Felsentaube*

Hindi: रॉक कबूतर

Indonesian: *Merpati batu*

Italian: *Piccione selvatico*

Persian: کبوتر چاهی

Scots: *Calman creige*

Spanish: *Paloma brava*

Swahili: *Njiwa-mjini*

Thai: นกพิราบป่า

evolutionary theorist Charles Darwin loved them, too. He kept and bred his own flock, and they helped inspire his ideas about evolution.

And then there's the case of Nikola Tesla, famous inventor and lovelorn pigeon nurse. Tesla fed crumbs to pigeons from the window of his home at New York's Hotel Pennsylvania. Whenever a sick pigeon would appear at his sill, he'd capture it and send it to the ASPCA Animal Hospital for care. His relationship with one particular white bird was "the love story of Tesla's life," according to his biographer John J. O'Neill. "Yes, I loved that pigeon," Tesla told O'Neill. "I loved her as a man loves a woman, and she loved me. As long as I had her, there was a purpose in my life." (Which is . . . certainly something.) When the pigeon passed away, Tesla felt that purpose leave him.

What's so special about pigeons, and why do people fall head over heels for them? This book answers the question. You'll discover that pigeons are behaviorally bizarre (they feed milk to their young), anatomically fascinating (they have three eyelids and lungs that don't expand), and historically compelling (they were so deeply involved in class struggles that they could have starred in *Les Misérables*). You'll also gain all the tools you need to become a pigeon watcher. If you're a pigeon hater, this book could change your mind. And who knows— maybe you'll even fall in love.

10 REASONS TO WATCH PIGEONS

1) It's free.

2) Pigeons are often easy to find, especially in urban areas where other wildlife is scarce. You can watch them on long drives, during boring commutes, or on lunch breaks. If you're in a dull meeting, take a peek outside and enjoy the soap opera of pigeon life.

3) Pigeons are gentle and safe to watch, so long as you look out for their poop. They won't attack you, screech at you, or spray you with a noxious scent. (If they do, you have misidentified your pigeons.)

4) They do strange and wonderful things. They blink with three eyelids, kiss with vigor, feed milk to their babies, and applaud themselves after sex. Their lives are both alarmingly alien and charmingly familiar.

5) If you're searching for dating tips, look no further than a species that mates for life (usually) and dances to impress.

6) Pigeons are food for many birds of prey. If you can find pigeons, you can find majestic hawks, falcons, owls, and all sorts of other shy aerial predators. The more you watch these birds, the more you'll appreciate the full breadth of nature that's quietly making a living all around you.

7) Thanks to some fascinating genetics, pigeons come in a variety of colors, patterns, and plumages. You'll find birds with funny feathery socks, odd-colored eyes, and dazzling hues from red to blue to white. Try to spot them all!

8) As our domesticated companions for millennia, pigeons have a lot to teach us about human history and culture. If given the power to speak, any pigeon could teach a master class on colonialism, inequality, architecture, agriculture, and changing food preferences.

9) Rescued pigeons make great pets—and if you're concerned about poop, you can dress your pigeon in a custom-made rhinestone-studded diaper. Seriously.

10) It's a hard world. Sometimes you just need to look at a soft bird.

They'll steal your crumbs . . . and your heart.

BASIC PIGEONOLOGY

Why Pigeons Are Dinosaurs, Doves, and Puppies

What is a pigeon? Where did the name "pigeon" come from? Who are a pigeon's closest relatives, and why are there pigeons everywhere? Before you start watching these birds in earnest, you need to know what the heck you're looking at. Here's a quick pigeon primer.

PIGEONS ARE DINOSAURS

It's true. Pigeons are birds, and birds evolved from dinosaurs—more specifically, from a group of dinosaurs called theropods, of which *Tyrannosaurus rex* is the most famous member. If you want to see incontrovertible evidence of this bird-dino connection, look to the exquisitely preserved fossils of feather-coated dinosaurs that paleontologists began to unearth in China in the 1990s. Chickens, sparrows, parrots, crows, and all the other birds we see around us every day are dinosaurs as well, scientifically speaking. We live in *Jurassic Park*. (Hold on to your butts.)

Pigeons and dinosaurs share another special connection. Many dinosaurs had two feathery wings. But back in the Cretaceous period, certain dinos, known as microraptorians, had four "wings": Their legs sprouted asymmetrical wing-like feathers that may have helped them glide. Though the microraptorians are extinct, some fancy pigeon breeds—like

Dinos walk among us.

the beautifully named fairy swallows—are able to grow wing feathers on their legs. It's as if pigeons and dinosaurs are high-fiving each other across the mists of time.

Scientists aren't sure when the first pigeons strutted onto the scene. Birds emerged in the Jurassic period, some 150 million years ago. There aren't many ancient pigeons in the fossil record, but DNA evidence suggests that the earliest pigeons may have evolved roughly 60 million years ago, six million years after a catastrophic asteroid strike wiped out so many of the critters we associate with dinosaur times. The age of non-bird dinos was over, but the glorious reign of the pigeons had just begun.

PIGEONS ARE DOVES

Try this: Think about what the words "pigeon" and "dove" mean to you. Many people think of pigeons as dirty and doves as peaceful, elegant, and even holy. But you've been fooled by Big Dove. Technically speaking, pigeons and doves are the same thing.

All species of pigeons and doves belong to a scientific family of birds called Columbidae. What's a scientific family? Here's a refresher from biology class: Scientists split living things into groups based on what they're related to. There are groupings within groupings, nested like a set of Russian dolls. A *species* is a group of very closely related living things that can breed with each other and make offspring that can breed, too. You belong to the species *Homo sapiens*. A group of closely related species is called a *genus* (plural, *genera*). Neanderthals and other early humans were part of the genus *Homo*. A group of genera is called a *family*. Humans belong to the great ape family, along with chimps, orangutans, and gorillas. A group of families is called an *order* . . . and there are larger and larger groupings until you get to the largest and most basic group: all living things.

Pigeons and doves all fall within the Columbidae family, but inside that family, there's no real distinction between the birds we call pigeons and those we label doves. They're not two separate groups, genetically or evolutionarily speaking. In general, people tend to call the bigger members of Columbidae pigeons and the smaller, daintier birds doves, but there are plenty of exceptions. Consider the hefty wompoo fruit-dove,

Yup, there's no difference.

which can measure 18 inches (46 cm) in length, longer than a loaf of bread. Then there's the wee dwarf fruit-dove, which can be 6 inches (15 cm) long, about the length of a dollar bill. Plus, the "doves" that we release at weddings are either white domesticated rock pigeons or white domesticated ring-necked doves. Most people can't tell the difference. (Don't release doves. When we toss these gentle pets into unfamiliar surroundings, they tend to starve, get hit by cars, or succumb to predators.)

Since there's no evolutionary distinction between the birds called pigeons and those called doves, these aren't scientifically valid categories. So, why the heck does English have two different words for the same bird? The confusion may date back to the Norman conquest of England in 1066. The invading Normans spoke French, so once they arrived, French words began to work their way into the English language. The word "pigeon" is French and originates from the classical Latin word *pīpiāre*, meaning "chirp" or "cheep." "Dove," on the other hand, has Old English, Norse, and German roots and may come from a word for "dive" or "dip," perhaps a reference to the birds' head bobbing or their ability to dive through the air. As English-speaking people encountered various species of doves and pigeons, they named them one or the other, somewhat indiscriminately. What a mess. Pigeons/doves aren't the only critters that have two names in English, one coming from French. For example, the word "cow" has English roots, but slaughtered cows become beef (from the French *boeuf*).

THE PIGEON FAMILY IS WEIRD AND WONDERFUL

Regardless of what you call them, the members of the family Columbidae are diverse and amazing. They share some general characteristics: These species tend to have short, skinny beaks, stubby necks, and stout bodies, and many of them build messy, haphazard nests and eat fruit or seeds. But they come in a mind-blowing variety of colors, shapes, and sizes. Here are a few of the strangest species.

Dodo

Yes, the world's most famous extinct bird was a flightless pigeon. Poor dodos don't deserve their reputation as slow, stupid birds—they were agile, and their flightless wings were muscular, possibly helping them maintain their balance as they ran through the forest.

Nicobar Pigeon

The dodo's likely closest living relative is also the world's most spectacular pigeon, the glam rocker of Columbidae. Native to southeast Asia, it's an iridescent rainbow of a bird. A long mane of plumes spills down from its storm-gray head. Just wow.

Galápagos Dove

The Galápagos Islands are full of animals found nowhere else—including a unique pigeon. The Galápagos dove has striking blue eyeliner, rosy legs, and a streaky brown body. It munches on seeds, insects, and cactus blossoms.

Victoria Crowned-Pigeon

This is one of the heftiest pigeon species, weighing up to nearly 5.33 pounds (2.4 kg). It's also one of the fanciest, with dark eyeliner and a crest like an exquisitely sewn doily. It lives in New Guinea, where its population is declining because of habitat loss and poaching.

Laughing Dove

The laughing dove's call sounds like someone going "woo-hoo-HOO-hoo-hoo!" But the reason for its chortling is deadly serious: It's trying to woo a mate. The laughing dove is an abundant, commonly seen bird, laughing it up across Africa and parts of Asia.

LOL

Kererū

A New Zealand species, the kererū is a colorful, portly bird that loves to eat fruit from native plants like mahoe and non-native species like cherries. Sometimes the fruit ferments inside its crop, and the bird gets drunk on its own homebrewed alcohol. It can get so intoxicated that it passes out and falls from its perch. Wildlife care centers often become inundated with inebriated birds brought in by concerned citizens.

Orange Dove

Found in Fiji, this striking bird looks like a huge ripe orange with a tiny lime on top. It mostly eats fruit, so maybe it's also fruit-flavored? (Please don't eat it.) The orange dove's peculiar call sounds like a metronome ticking away.

Luzon Bleeding-Heart

Like other bleeding-heart doves, this species looks like it's been shot through the heart (and you're to blame). But that red patch is made of feathers, not blood. Native to the Philippines, the Luzon bleeding-heart dove is shy and hard to spot in the wild. All of the bleeding-heart doves are threatened with extinction; the Luzon bleeding-heart is the least endangered.

Sadly, about a third of the members of Columbidae are in trouble, threatened by overhunting and our insatiable appetite for land. But there's one species of pigeon that you'll see almost everywhere you go. It's a stout-bodied bird with plumage that varies from white to brick red to gray to black. You'll find it in big cities and under highway overpasses. You'll spot it in rural areas, especially where there's grain to eat. It lives on every continent except Antarctica. And it's the topic of this book.

Let's home in on this special bird.

MEET *THE* PIGEON

So, what should we call this bird? It really depends on who you ask. English-speaking people call it by several names, including rock pigeon (since it sometimes lives on rocky cliffs), rock dove (since pigeons are also doves), and common pigeon (because it's common, which is accurate but honestly so bland). Bird enthusiasts frequently engage in heated debates about the "right" name. The American Ornithological Society, which compiles the official bird checklists of North and Middle America, currently goes with rock pigeon. A 2018 proposal to change the name to rock dove (to avoid confusion with an Australian bird called the rock pigeon) was struck down, but not before ruffling some feathers.

Our hero.

This problem isn't limited to pigeons. Many other plants and animals have a slew of common names. Consider the large brown North American mammal that burrows in soil and eats your garden plants: In English, you'd call it the groundhog, or, alternately, the woodchuck, wood-schock, whistle pig, whistler, red monk, Canada marmot, thickwood badger, or, amazingly, land beaver. And there are plenty of non-English names, too. Whoof.

Scientists, in a desperate attempt to bring some clarity to this classification problem, developed their own naming system called binomial nomenclature. These "scientific names" consist of two words. The first word is the name of the critter's genus, and the second is the specific epithet, which distinguishes that species within the genus. To make these scientific names stand out from common names, scientists write them in italics, with the first word capitalized, *Like this*. So, when the German naturalist Johann Friedrich Gmelin first provided an extensive scientific description of the pigeon in 1789, he called it:

Columba livia

Fancy, right? The genus name *Columba* comes from the Latin word for dove. The species name *livia* refers to its dark, leaden hue. As scientific names go, it's not bad. It's clear, descriptive, and pretty easy to pronounce. (This isn't always the case. Consider the critter with the longest scientific name, the myxobacterium *Myxococcus llanfairpwllgwyngyllgogery-chwyrndrobwllllantysiliogogogochensis*, which recently edged out the fly *Parastratiosphecomyia stratiosphecomyioides* for longest on the books. Or ponder purely hilarious names like the beetle *Agra vation* and the snail *Ba humbugi*.)

So, this book focuses on the species *Columba livia*, but let's keep things simple and step away from the Latin. Many people just call *Columba livia* "the pigeon," since it's the pigeon species that most people see. That's how we'll refer to it from here on out: **the pigeon**. Just don't forget that it's not the only pigeon; it's *Columba livia*, one of many species in a big, beautiful pigeon family.

PIGEONS ARE PUPPIES

If you're a dog owner, you've heard this story. Once upon a time, thousands and thousands of years ago—we're not exactly sure when, or whether it happened multiple times—some wolves hung out near humans and slowly turned into domestic dogs. Humans chose wolves with particularly desirable traits (gentleness, or protectiveness, or strange-looking fur) and bred them together to produce a variety of groupings, or breeds, that shared common characteristics. Nowadays, dogs come in hundreds of breeds, from tiny Chihuahuas to powerful rottweilers to curly-haired poodles. Most of them are a far cry from those rugged ancient wolves, especially when we dress them in little tutus.

Who's a good pupper?

The story of pigeons is pretty much the same. Thousands of years ago in the Fertile Crescent, some folks realized that pigeons were easy to care for. Again, we're not exactly sure where or when this happened, and it probably happened multiple times. But we do know that these pigeon-keeping people built special houses where pigeons could nest. They chose birds that had desirable traits (meatiness, or gentleness, or pretty feathers) and mated them together, developing hundreds of breeds to serve all sorts of purposes.

For most of us, these varieties are less familiar than dog breeds, but they're no less weird and wonderful: the droopy-faced scandaroon, the enormous American giant runt, the goofy-sounding Thai laugher. As with dog evolution, most pure-bred birds are a far cry from those rugged ancient pigeons, especially when we dress them in rhinestone diapers. (We really do this—see page 196.)

As these pigeon-loving people have traveled over millennia, they've taken their birds with them. They even carried them to new continents; European settlers brought pigeons to North America at the start of the seventeenth century. Wherever pigeons went, some of them escaped. That wasn't unexpected—domesticated animals often run loose and set up thriving "wild" populations. We have a word for these creatures: ferals. The world is full of feral dogs, cats, pigs, horses, and goats. Pigeons followed the same path. When they escaped, they didn't go far; bred to live alongside humans, they nested on our houses and ate our grain and trash. It was what they knew.

OTHER FERAL FAUNA

- Cats released on islands have contributed to the extinction of many birds, such as the island of Réunion's portly Réunion pink pigeon, driven to extinction around 1700.
- Dogs have learned to ride Moscow's subway system, begging for treats and pats from riders.
- Donkeys, descendants of the African ass, wander the American West.
- Rabbits were intentionally set free on Japan's Okunoshima Island, the former site of a chemical weapons plant, and they now attract tons of tourists.
- Water buffalo were introduced to Australia, where they trample and muddy precious wetlands.

Here's the most mind-blowing thing about feral pigeons: Their history explains why they come in so many different colors. See, feral dogs vary in color because they're a blend of different breeds. Free of the pressures of human-directed breeding, they make all sorts of beautiful mutts. Feral pigeons are the same. Their grays, reds, browns, whites, and blacks are an expression of their complex heritage. Some of them even retain extravagant domestic traits like feathery feet or crests.

But there's one massive difference between feral dogs and feral pigeons. Most of us know that feral dogs were once pets. But we've forgotten why our cities, towns, and farms are packed with pigeons. We consider them pests. We trap them, shoot them, and hurl perhaps the ultimate insult at them: We call them "rats with wings." Ouch. (Sorry, rats.)

So, how did pigeons go from puppies to pests? Here is their story.

THE PASSION AND THE POOP

A History of Pigeons and People

The tale of pigeons and people is a wild ride. Pigeons have coexisted with humans for thousands of years—and because of this long-lasting relationship, the history of pigeons has all the twists and turns of human drama. There's heroism, war, royalty, and revolution. And crap. So much crap.

FROM WILD TO DOMESTIC

Before pigeons flocked to our streets, they nested in caverns on rocky cliffs in parts of northern Africa, southern Europe, the northern British Isles, and western Asia. Some still do; if you travel to rugged places like the remote seaside coasts of western Scotland, for example, you'll see pigeons swooping to and from the crags like they did in olden times (though it's hard to say if these are pure "wild" birds or if they've all got some feral DNA).

Our relatives, the now-extinct Neanderthals, may have been the world's earliest pigeon fans. Archaeologists have uncovered roughly 67,000-year-old pigeon bones from a cave in Gibraltar that show cut marks and signs of burning, indicating that Neanderthals were butchering and preparing the birds for food. The cave holds evidence of at least 40,000 years (!) of pigeon meals.

At some point, a few pigeons said goodbye to the wild and became our partners. How did this happen? Did a single, lonely human slowly

A wild pigeon's world.

earn the trust of a friendly pigeon on a windswept beach? Did this human tentatively stretch out her hand to pat the pigeon's beak in a poignant moment of connection and mutual understanding? Sadly, no. Domestication is a complicated, messy process, and its first steps probably weren't even intentional.

About 12,000 years ago, people in the area of the Middle East known as the Fertile Crescent began to build permanent settlements for themselves and farm the land. They created a new kind of habitat, and some animals took advantage of it. Pigeons settled in to breed in and around these dwellings and munch on spilled grain. People began, in turn, to eat the pigeons. They built pigeon houses and selectively bred birds that had desirable traits.

Of course, it's hard to narrow down exactly when this happened; early records are hard to come by (we're getting back to the dawn of recorded writing here). Ancient Egyptians were eating pigeons by the early third millennium BCE, and Sumerian administrative texts from the late third millennium refer to domesticated pigeons. There probably wasn't one "aha" moment of domestication; much like the development of agriculture, it happened many different times and in many different places. That's because pigeons are shockingly, deeply useful.

WAIT—WHY THE HECK DID PEOPLE DOMESTICATE PIGEONS?

Watch a flock of pigeons pecking at the crumbs from a discarded, run-over bag of neon-orange chips and you might not immediately sense how these birds could come in handy. For many of our other domesticated animal companions, it's fairly obvious why we brought them into our homes or farms. Domesticated dogs keep us company and guard our property. Domesticated horses carry us around. Domesticated sheep give us wool, skins, meat, and cheese. Domesticated cats keep our reflexes sharp by knocking our water glasses off the table. Domesticated pigeons are good at . . . cooing . . . okay, what do they do for us, exactly?

First off, pigeons are edible. If you find the idea of eating pigeons unappealing *but* you consume chicken, then you're a product of a particular time, place, and culture. Do you live in the United States or Europe? Before the days of factory-farmed chickens, people in these places ate tons of pigeon. Squab, the tender meat from young birds that are about to leave the nest, was particularly prized. Pigeon meat is still highly popular in many parts of the world. In Egypt, for example, people celebrate special occasions by eating hamam mahshi, a dish of squab stuffed with spiced rice or freekeh.

At one time, the skies over parts of North America were filled with tasty pigeons native to the continent: passenger pigeons. In the 1800s, they numbered perhaps 3 to 5

The passenger pigeon.

The species served as a valuable food for many American Indians. The Seneca people call the passenger pigeon jah'gowa, "big bread," because it was such an abundant source of nourishment. But the arrival of European colonists spelled doom for these birds. In the mid-1800s, the combination of new railway lines and growing cities full of hungry inhabitants led to massive commercial overharvesting and the destruction of nesting habitat. The last passenger pigeon, a bird named Martha, died in a zoo in 1914.

Pigeons provide meat, but they offer something else that's valuable: poop. It's not just a mess—it's brown-and-white gold. Rich in nitrogen, the dung is a potent crop fertilizer. It also

Precious poop.

plays a role in some traditional processes for making leather: Animal hides are steeped in fermented feces to soften them. Plus, pigeon poop is a source of saltpeter, one of the three key components (along with sulfur and charcoal) of gunpowder.

Meat and poop are only the beginning—the tip of the beak, if you will. We've also bred pigeons to be companions and show animals. We've raced them against each other and strapped important messages to their legs. We've used them for scientific research and for target practice; the 1900 Olympic Games in Paris featured a grisly live pigeon shoot. We've attached lights and whistles to them so they make art and music when they fly.

Of course, lots of animals seem useful at first but less so upon reflection. A giraffe could reach the top shelf in your kitchen and a tiger could intimidate your pals when you play poker, but domestication of these creatures would be, to put it mildly, a challenge. Pigeons, on the other hand, are just very domesticate-able. Relatively gentle and harmless, they can survive on a spoonful or two of cheap grain per day, plus veggies a few days per week. Pigeon keepers can let their birds out to forage and expect them to come back to their nests at night. Pigeons don't migrate; they prefer to stick around our settlements year-round. And they breed like rabbits. They can start reproducing at just six months old and make babies throughout the year, even in the coldest months, so long as they've got access to food.

With all of these perks, pigeon domestication was a foregone conclusion. Let's take a look at some of those first pigeon keepers.

PIGEONS IN EARLY RELIGION, ART, AND FOOD

The earliest history of pigeon keeping is murky because it happened a long time ago—perhaps long before the dawn of recorded writing. Archaeologists have uncovered ancient artifacts from the Fertile Crescent that look like pigeons, but there's a catch: It's not clear whether these pieces of art portray wild pigeons, domesticated pigeons, or some altogether different species. For example, we've got a beautiful flint sculpture of a pigeon-like bird from Egypt's predynastic period (4400 to 3100 BCE). But it's a rough piece, without any color or other subtle details that might enable us to narrow down the species. Another piece of pigeon-y Egyptian art comes from between 3100 and 2600 BCE; it's a vessel carved from red stone, shaped like a very pudgy pigeon of some kind, but again, which pigeon? (It sure is cute, though.)

If we move a little forward in time, we find a lot more evidence for the importance of pigeons in ancient Egypt, including tombs decorated with elegant paintings of birds that look just like today's feral pigeons. A funeral meal preserved in a tomb from the Second Dynasty (about 2800 to 2675 BCE) features a pigeon stew. And King Ramses III, who ruled from roughly 1186 to 1155 BCE, sacrificed a whopping 57,810 of the birds to the god Amon at Thebes over the course of his reign.

Our early relationship with pigeons wasn't just bloody. We worshipped them. We admired their peacefulness, their loyalty to their mates, and their propensity for having lots and lots and lots of babies. They became symbols for many early

Red breccia vessel in the form of a bird,
after an object in the British Museum.

goddesses, including the Mesopotamian goddess Inanna, the Canaanite goddesses Asherah and Astarte, and the Greek goddess Aphrodite.

The Torah and the Bible are also full of pigeons. Sure, there's plenty of bird murder—the book of Leviticus, for example, contains helpful instructions on how to sacrifice pigeons to cure skin disease. And in the New Testament, Mary and Joseph offer pigeons for sacrifice after Jesus is born. But the birds are also a symbol of peace and hope. After the great flood, Noah releases a dove (a.k.a. a pigeon!) to find out if the waters have receded enough to reveal land. Later, the Holy Spirit appears as a dove to celebrate the baptism of Jesus by John the Baptist. And the romantic Song of Songs uses the pigeon as a saucy metaphor for a loved one: "O my dove, in the clefts of the rock, in the crannies of the cliff, let me see your face." Whether or not you interpret this as a risqué allegory, you can't deny that it's an accurate description of pigeon habitat.

PIGEON PALACES

If you want to raise a lot of pigeons—enough to, say, sacrifice thousands of them to your favorite god—you need a special kind of structure. Pigeons don't thrive in chicken coops or parrot cages. They nest in holes in cliffs, so you must build your own indoor cliff, a structure called a dovecote.

What does this kind of indoor cliff look like? Let's examine one of the earliest known dovecotes, dating from roughly 800 to 500 BCE. Discovered in Jordan, in an arid, rocky landscape near a highway, it's a round underground structure hewn directly into the limestone. Its walls are riddled with carved, squarish cavities that served as nesting caves. With hundreds of cavities in all, the whole thing looks like a honeycomb for absurdly big bees.

Clearly, Iron Age pigeon keeping was a major operation. At another site in the region, this one in Palestine, archaeologists have found a complex of sixty dovecotes. Altogether, they have

DOVECOTE DECOR

Though some dovecotes are freestanding, others are attached to buildings as wall-mounted structures, gables, or even extra floors. If you own a sprawling country mansion, consider affixing a bespoke dovecote to your rustic barn and inviting your local pigeon-loving author over for tea.

an unfathomable 50,000 to 60,000 nesting holes. This type of large-scale pigeon keeping meant that people could easily collect lots of pigeon poop, and pigeon poop helped put food on the table. In some parts of the Middle East, the dung was a vitally important fertilizer for crops, especially in places where the

Life inside a dovecote.

soil was poor and needed regular input of nutrients. So, pigeons provided protein for dinner *and* nourished the fruits and veggies served alongside it.

Those first dovecotes were impressively big, but they weren't fancy. That was about to change. As pigeon keeping intensified and spread, dovecotes became palaces. Visit Palestrina, Italy, and you can see a gorgeous mosaic from the first century BCE that depicts a multitiered dovecote stretching into the sky next to the Egyptian Nile. In the sixteenth century in England, Sir John Gostwick, lord of Willington Manor, built a spectacular limestone dovecote rising more than three stories high. This miniature castle has an elegant two-tiered tiled roof and can hold 3,000 birds. It still stands strong today, a stunning testament to craftsmanship (and probably also to Sir Gostwick's luck in being well-liked by the murderous King Henry VIII). In sixteenth- and seventeenth-century Iran, where pigeon poop was an essential fertilizer for melons and cucumbers, dovecotes could reach more than six stories high. Their rounded, honeycombed interiors fit up to 14,000 birds. Each nesting hole was cut with geometric precision. Today, you can step inside these vast towers and look up into a dizzying, kaleidoscopic pattern of cavities.

Dovecotes weren't just barns for livestock. They were works of art. And this art was bankrolled by the super-rich. Whereas today's wealthy elites buy private jets and private islands, history's mega-rich splurged on private pigeons.

COOP D'ÉTAT

Royals from France to Iran to India were pigeon-obsessed. Al-Muzaffar Hajji, a sultan of the Bahri Mamluk dynasty in fourteenth-century Egypt, reared pigeons and bet huge amounts of gold and pearls on high-stakes pigeon races. In nineteenth-century England, Queen Victoria doted on her collection of fancy pigeons, and she had a particular fondness for the hooded breed known as Jacobins (learn more about them on page 96). And perhaps the world's most impressive pigeon keeper was the Mughal emperor Akbar, who ruled over parts of South Asia in the mid-sixteenth and early seventeenth century. He bred pigeons for various qualities such as fancy flying, attractive hues, and interesting voices (some birds were said to sound like the Muslim call to prayer). Akbar kept more than 20,000 pigeons at his court, and when he traveled, his servants carried along his favorite birds in portable dovecotes.

For the Mughal emperors, these birds were more than just a fun hobby. They were statecraft. The emperors turned pigeon keeping from a popular pastime to a high-status sport, and they traded valuable birds to solidify political alliances. When Emperor Akbar entertained diplomats from afar, he wowed them by showing off his birds. As Akbar's grand vizier Abu'l-Fazl ibn Mubarak wrote, this was an attempt at psychological manipulation. Akbar used his display of pigeon prowess "as a way of reducing unsettled, worldly-minded men to obedience." Try bringing a flock of pigeons to your next important business meeting and see if you can score that sweet promotion!

Elites and pigeons went hand in wing, and in some places, this ruffled feathers. Pigeon keeping became a status symbol—and another convenient way to oppress the commoners. In France from the Middle Ages onward, only landowners were allowed to build dovecotes. The landowners' birds would fly down

The regal-looking Jacobin.

to peasants' fields and chow down on crops, but the commoners weren't permitted to kill these beaked bandits. Tensions mounted. When the French Revolution erupted, peasants gleefully marched up to lordly dovecotes and smashed them. On August 4, 1789, France's National Constituent Assembly decreed an end to feudalism and declared that the lords no longer had exclusive rights to pigeons.

The situation was also dire in England. During the sixteenth and seventeenth centuries, feudal lords struggled to one-up each other by building bigger, more elaborate dovecotes. (You know what they say about a lord with a big dovecote.) By the middle of the seventeenth century, there were perhaps 26,000 dovecotes in England. But these structures were under a bizarre threat, one that went all the way to the top. The monarchy was desperate to stockpile tons of gunpowder to fuel its many wars. One of gunpowder's key ingredients,

DICKENSIAN DOVECOTES

In Charles Dickens's novel about the French Revolution, *A Tale of Two Cities*, a dying peasant boy lists dovecotes among his grievances against a marquis: The peasants are "obliged to feed scores of [the marquis's] tame birds on our wretched crops, and forbidden for our lives to keep a single tame bird of our own."

saltpeter, is found in pigeon poop. Royals sent poop collectors called saltpetermen to barge into dovecotes and seize all the precious dung. In the process, the saltpetermen often damaged or knocked down the structures, causing much rage among the landowning class. (They also destroyed churches, town halls, barns, outhouses, and any other buildings whose soil was rich in human and other mammalian excrement, *and* they used saucy language while they were at it.)

While landowners and royals fought over bird crap, commoners looked on wistfully. Just as in France, ordinary English folks weren't allowed to keep pigeons. Commoners who built secret, illicit dovecotes were forced to destroy them. Fortunately, by the mid-1600s, this social prohibition eased up, even if the law remained unchanged until the early nineteenth century. Everyday people took to pigeon keeping with great enthusiasm—and it helped lead to one of the most important scientific breakthroughs of all time.

DARWIN'S PIGEON PALS

When we think about Charles Darwin's work with birds, we tend to picture him peering at the Galápagos Islands' various finches and noting the subtle variations in their beaks. But finches weren't the only birds that helped Charles Darwin formulate his world-shaking theory of natural selection. He made some of his greatest discoveries while knee-deep (really, ankle-deep) in pigeons.

The finches of the Galápagos were cool and all, but in 1855, Darwin was searching for some type of animal that he could breed and study at home in England. Pigeon keeping was all the rage in the Victorian era, so pigeons seemed the obvious choice. Darwin rolled up his sleeves and built a dovecote in his garden. Then he packed it with the fanciest pigeons he could find. He went to pigeon shows, hung out with keepers, and learned how to talk pigeon with the best of them. And he fell head over heels in love.

In a letter to his geologist pal Charles Lyell on November 4, 1855, Darwin wrote, with all the creepy glee of a biologist, "I am deeply immersed on the subject of Pigeons, & have pairs of seven or eight kinds alive & am watching them outside & then shall skeletonise them & watch their insides." Fun! He urged Lyell to visit, wooing him with the promise of a tour of his dovecote, "the greatest treat, in my opinion, which can be offered to [a] human being."

Darwin kept some of the world's weirdest pigeon breeds: dragoons, fantails, scandaroons, tumblers, and many more. He had birds with teensy beaks, fan-shaped tails, fleshy eye rings, and other surprising traits. As Darwin observed (and doted on) his birds, he waded into a controversial issue in the pigeon world. At the time, plenty of pigeon breeders were certain that each unique breed descended from its own species. But many naturalists disagreed; they suspected that all pigeons descended from one species. Darwin soon noted certain

Charles Darwin adored pigeons.

similarities and he became convinced that one single species had given rise to all those odd-looking breeds.

This idea became a key part of his 1859 book, *On the Origin of Species*. In the pigeon-filled first chapter, Darwin wrote, "Great as the differences are between the breeds of the pigeon, I am fully convinced that the common opinion of naturalists is correct, namely, that all are descended from the rock-pigeon (*Columba livia*)." Darwin believed that the way people shaped pigeons into different breeds was similar to the way that nature shapes species in the wild, producing an endless variety of weird forms. The lowly feral pigeon, fishing the last crumbs out of that chip bag, is a microcosm of the natural world.

THE PIGEONTERNET

Back in 1850, when Charles Darwin had yet to release *On the Origin of Species*—and was working on several significantly less popular books about barnacles—a German businessman was putting pigeons to a more pedestrian use. His name was Israel Beer Josaphat, but he later changed it to Paul Julius Reuter. Yes, *that* Reuter, founder of a media empire.

At the time, Europe was buzzing with a new, exciting communication system: the telegraph. It was fast and efficient but relied on cables, and in some places the telegraph cable network was pretty patchy. Reuter identified a critical communication bottleneck: a 76-mile (122 km) gap in the cables between Brussels, Belgium, and Aachen, Germany. He knew exactly how to fill it: with pigeons.

Reuter procured some birds and used them to carry information between Brussels and Aachen. The system was highly successful. After about a year, however, cables were strung across the gap in the line, and Reuter ended his pigeon messenger service. But he was well on his way to media fame.

Pigeons are great at carrying messages. If you transport a trusty pigeon far from its home loft, affix a note to its leg, chest, or back, and release it, it'll bring your message home quickly— flying at about 60 miles per hour (97 kph)—and with remarkable accuracy. It'll even do this over long distances; some birds can fly up to 600 miles (966 km) or more. Early messages were just rolls of paper tied to a pigeon with string. Later messages were inserted into hollow goose quills, then elegant metal capsules with twist-off lids, followed by plastic capsules with fabric ties and metal snaps.

Of course, this method has its limits. A messenger pigeon is only interested in flying in one direction: back home. If you want to send a reply, you can't use the same bird; no amount of pleading will convince it to abandon its mate and its warm, cozy loft. Instead, you need to attach your new message to a second bird whose loft is back at the first message's origin point. It's a little trickier than email, but once you've got a system in place, it works beautifully.

Pigeons were the original internet. They could update you on political news or give you the latest sports scores. Ancient Romans relied on them to carry critical wartime intelligence and spread the outcomes of chariot races. In 776 BCE, pigeons delivered the results of the very first Olympic Games. In the

PIGEON NAVIGATION

When you drop off a pigeon in an unfamiliar location, it usually finds its way home. But how? Scientists have uncovered clues, but nobody's unraveled the whole story yet. A pigeon likely uses a whole bag of tricks, including smelling the air, looking for familiar landmarks, observing the sun's position, detecting the Earth's magnetic field, and more. Different pigeons have their own personal navigational preferences.

PIGEON WHISTLES

Pigeons can carry more than words. In some parts of Asia, including China, Japan, and Indonesia, there's a longstanding tradition of crafting whistles and strapping them to pigeons' tails. When the birds fly, wind flows through the whistles, making airy, ethereal sounds. A good pigeon whistle maker must balance elaborate designs and tonal quality with the weight load limits of the birds—the extreme upper limit of a pigeon's carrying ability is 4.4 ounces (0.125 kg), and it can haul this load across only a few meters. Pigeon whistles are made of bamboo, dried gourd, and other featherlight material, and they come in a dizzying variety of sizes and designs. They're music, sculpture, tradition, and pigeon keeping rolled into one.

twelfth century CE, Genghis Khan set up a relay network of birds across Asia and parts of eastern Europe. And during the Franco-Prussian War of 1870–71, the people of Paris, besieged and cut off from the rest of the world, turned to a truly steampunk solution. Hot-air balloon pilots loaded their baskets with pigeons and took to the skies. Once they'd navigated their way out of Paris and over to friendly territory, they brought their loyal birds to a government outpost. Officials attached intel and personal letters (on microfiche, the dusty favorite of libraries everywhere) to the pigeons' tails and sent them back home.

Pigeon heroism flew to new heights during World Wars I and II. The birds were a serious tactical advantage. They carried messages through the nightmarish landscape of trench warfare, braving enemy fire and toxic gas and saving thousands of soldiers' lives.

World War I's most famous pigeon war hero was Cher Ami (French for "Dear Friend"). In October 1918, US soldiers from the Seventy-Seventh Division—also known as the Lost Battalion—were advancing behind enemy lines in the Argonne Forest of northeast France when enemy maneuvers trapped them. Surrounded and stuck, they fell under friendly artillery fire. In desperation, they loosed a messenger pigeon, but in the chaos, they forgot to attach a note. They released a second bird, their dear friend Cher Ami. He rose up into the sky, taking

Cher Ami

their hopes with him—and, to their horror, he was shot before their eyes. The soldiers were out of pigeons and out of luck.

But wait! Against all odds, and despite sustaining grievous injuries to his leg and breast, Cher Ami made it back to headquarters. He delivered this message: "We are along the road parallel 276.4. Our artillery is dropping a barrage directly on us. For heaven's sake, stop it." That day's artillery fire had already ended, but when the next day's barrage began, it avoided the battalion. For his bravery, Cher Ami was showered with praise and press attention. He received the Croix de Guerre, one of France's highest military honors, as well as a gold medal from the Organized Bodies of American Pigeon Fanciers.

Here, reporting for duty, are a few more of the many decorated war hero pigeons:

Mary of Exeter

During World War II, spies working for the Allies carried Mary behind enemy lines into France. They affixed critical intelligence to the bird and released her to return to her loft in Exeter, England, which stood behind the boot  workshop of her owner, Cecil "Charlie" Brewer. Despite sustaining severe injuries from shrapnel, shotgun pellets, and a hungry bird of prey, she never failed a mission.

GI Joe

In 1943, a British brigade liberated an Italian town ahead of schedule. They knew that Americans planned to bomb the village, so they sent GI Joe in a last-ditch effort to call off the air raid. The bird delivered the message and saved the lives of more than a thousand soldiers.

Paddy

Born in Northern Ireland, Paddy carried critical intel from Normandy to England on June 12, 1944. He clocked the fastest pigeon flight time during the Normandy landings, zooming 230 miles (370 km) in just four hours and fifty minutes.

Winkie

In 1942, a Royal Air Force bomber went down in the North Sea. Its desperate crew released their messenger pigeon, Winkie. The bird flew 120 miles (193 km) home to her owner, who notified the RAF. Winkie wasn't carrying the plane's coordinates, but,

incredibly, the RAF was able to use her arrival time and the wind direction to calculate the plane's position. The soldiers were quickly and successfully rescued.

Pigeons were indescribably important, both to the war effort and to everyday life. In 1941, Wendell Mitchell Levi, former president of the National Pigeon Association, wrote in his much-celebrated tome *The Pigeon*, "Wherever civilization has flourished, there the pigeon has thrived, and the higher the civilization, usually the higher the regard for the pigeon." (Levi was also the author of a highly practical yet ominously named book called *Making Pigeons Pay*.) But things were about to change. Pigeons had reached the zenith of their popularity, and they would soon take a dive.

In the years following the world wars, more advanced communication methods like radio (and, later, email) made messenger pigeons obsolete. In some isolated places, people still sent carrier pigeons back and forth; until recently, for example, police in the eastern Indian state of Odisha used pigeons to keep remote police stations in the loop. But for most of us, messenger pigeons became retro technology—and not retro cool, like a pair of '80s sunglasses. Retro uncool, like a fax machine. How did our love of pigeons turn to loathing?

HOW ARE YOUR PIGEONS?

In the northeastern part of Scotland, folks greet each other with "Foos yer doos?" That's Doric for "How are your pigeons?" and it's a way to ask someone how they're doing. A common response is "Aye peckin' away (Always pecking)!"

SOME PIGEON EXPRESSIONS

The word "pigeon" itself has picked up a lot of alternate meanings over time. It can refer to a cheater, a coward, a beloved person, somebody who is easily taken advantage of, somebody who gets a journalist's story to the public by carrying it across a border (which is wonderfully specific), or a grayish hue more formally known as **PANTONE 15-4704**. The word has also popped up in tons of odd expressions, including:

PIGEON'S BLOOD: A dark-red color that's often used to describe an especially coveted ruby

PIGEON DROP: Criminal slang for a scam in which a con artist pretends to have found some money and offers to give it to the victim for a small fee

PIGEON-EYED: Drunk

PIGEON-HEARTED, PIGEON-LIVERED: Cowardly

PIGEONHOLE: To label something or someone in a limited way

PIGEON PAIR: Twins of the opposite sex, or a pair of siblings of the opposite sex

PIGEON'S THROAT: A blue-green color like the shine of a pigeon's throat feathers

PIGEON-TOED: Having inward-pointing toes

PLUCK A PIGEON: To swindle somebody

PUT THE CAT AMONG THE PIGEONS: To say something that causes chaos and upsets a lot of people

STOOL PIGEON: A police informer

*Columba informus:
the stool pigeon.*

FLYING THE COOP

The first step in the downfall of pigeon PR occurred early on: Pigeons went feral. This happened pretty much as soon as the birds were domesticated. Ferals multiplied and persisted even in places where pigeon keeping died out.

As people from the Old World traveled abroad, they carried pigeons with them—and many other critters, too. Colonialism is not only socially and culturally devastating, but also makes a biological mess. Colonists hell-bent on "civilizing" the peoples and lands of the Americas imported cows, wheat, pigeons, and other livestock and crops in the sixteenth and seventeenth centuries. Of course, Indigenous North Americans already had ecosystem-compatible ways of producing food, and many

Time to go feral.

SOME OTHER PLANTS & ANIMALS INTRODUCED TO THE AMERICAS

Apples

Carrots

Chickens

Cows

Honey bees

House centipedes

House mice

House sparrows

Mute swans

Norway rats

Ring-necked pheasants

Silverfish

Starlings

Tumbleweeds (yes, the Wild West didn't originally have them)

Indigenous peoples had time-tested farming traditions, but these methods were largely ignored or actively disrupted. And then there were the accidentally imported organisms. Colonial expansion spread all sorts of dangers, including bedbugs and the pathogens that cause smallpox, measles, and Dutch elm disease.

The impacts of these imports differ widely. Some aren't too destructive—pet golden hamsters, for example, have not yet escaped their plastic balls to go feral in North America—but some are cataclysmic. What about feral pigeons? Because they tend to stick close to human habitation, their effect on wild spaces is relatively minor. That doesn't mean they're harmless, though. For instance, they were implicated in the spread of disease to the unique Galápagos dove, so they've been systematically eradicated from those islands.

Wherever colonists settled, feral pigeons thrived. Meanwhile, the practice of pigeon keeping began to fall out of favor, at least in a broad sense. Some folks do still raise birds for meat, and in certain places, the culture of pigeon keeping carries on; people bond and socialize over their shared love of the birds. Pigeon racing is a booming business in parts of Asia, including China, Indonesia, and the Philippines. In 2020, a Chinese buyer purchased a Belgian racing pigeon named New Kim for a jaw-dropping $1.9 million. And South Africa hosts the Million Dollar Pigeon Race, where the entry fee is a steep

FAST FACTS ON PIGEON RACING

Racing pigeons don't travel around a track or have tiny saddles and wee jockeys. They just fly home as fast as they can. Ahead of a race, pigeons are transported far from their lofts and released en masse. When a bird returns home, a device scans an RFID tag around its ankle, recording its flight time. During a race, pigeons can get lost, encounter bad weather, or succumb to predators, especially during the longest events. Because of these dangers, animal rights activists have mobilized in opposition to the sport.

$1,100 per bird. But pigeons just aren't as widely popular as they used to be. That's partly because they can't compete with technology. Messenger pigeons are no match for our modern telecommunication systems. Pigeon poop isn't as popular and widely available as industrially produced fertilizers. Factory-farmed chicken has pushed squab off the dinner plate, partly because pigeon chicks need special nurturing from their parents and are hard to raise on an industrial scale that would satisfy modern appetites. Pigeons have lost their usefulness. And when we stop thinking that animals are useful, we find it a whole lot easier to hate them.

Once the darlings of the rich, pigeons became signs of urban poverty and decay. Their reputation took a huge hit in 1963 when two New Yorkers died from a fungal infection called cryptococcal meningitis. A city official stoked panic when he declared that pigeons were at fault (they weren't), and that the deadly fungus was drifting through the air and into the lungs of all New Yorkers (it wasn't). Then, in a 1966 article in the *New York Times*, Parks Commissioner Thomas P. F. Hoving listed pigeons as one of the city's so-called social troubles, along with homelessness, alcoholism, and littering. The pigeon, he said, was "a rat with wings." That phrase went global in 1980 when Woody Allen famously used it in his movie *Stardust Memories*. Pigeons had morphed into rats.

The ratification of the pigeon.

Nowadays, many people work hard to destroy those once prized pigeons. They poison them, trap them, and shoot them. They use netting, spikes, and plastic owls to keep them away from human settlements, the very environment people have bred them for. They've forgotten why feral pigeons exist. And that's a tragedy. If you push aside any feelings of disgust and stare into a pigeon's beady orange eyes, you can instantly immerse yourself in history, nature, and animal behavior. What you find will stun you.

In her book *Victoria: The Biography of a Pigeon*, author Alice Renton shares her experience rescuing a bedraggled, abandoned baby pigeon from a London train station. As she and her family rear their young charge, Renton is gobsmacked to discover that the bird, dubbed Victoria, is social and complex. She pecks toes, rides on heads, and gleefully flies alongside the car. One night, Victoria fails to return home and

Renton is surprised by the depth of her devastation: "I wasn't aware until now that [Victoria] had gradually made herself an indispensable member of the family. She was, after all, only a pigeon."

Only a pigeon? In their rich and authoritative book *Feral Pigeons*, the scientists Richard F. Johnston and Marián Janiga break from their otherwise dry tone to exclaim that feral pigeons are "one of the masterpieces of nature." Like all masterpieces, they're remarkable to behold—if you know what to look for.

PIGEONATOMY

From Beak to Cloaca

Pigeons are weirder than they look at first glance. Once you know how they function—that they see ultraviolet, hear infrasound, blink with three eyelids, and can detect malignant tumors—you'll do a double take every time you spot one. Here are the ins and outs of pigeon anatomy.

OUTSIDE BITS

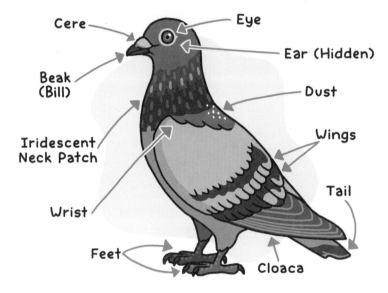

Cere

Eye

Ear (Hidden)

Beak
(Bill)

Dust

Iridescent
Neck Patch

Wings

Wrist

Tail

Feet

Cloaca

Selected outside bits.

Beak

A bird's beak has more in common with a cow's horns than with your teeth. It's a bony core overlaid with the same stuff that's in hair and nails: a protein called keratin. So why don't birds have teeth? Their dino ancestors had teeth, and so did the earliest birds, but modern birds don't—and scientists aren't sure why.

Some scientists propose an intriguing explanation involving embryos. If you're a tiny embryonic chick developing inside an egg, you must work hard and expend energy to grow all sorts of body parts. Teeth in particular take ages to grow. That's a problem, because a baby bird inside an egg is in terrible danger; eggs are basically delicious, defenseless packaged meals that a clever predator could easily steal. By skipping the tooth-growing process, a baby bird can spend less time inside an egg and emerge more quickly into its world. So, perhaps the pressures of predation robbed our birds of their teeth.

BILL OR BEAK?

If you refer to the pointy end of a bird as the "beak," someone might grumble, "Actually, it's called a bill." So which is correct, bill or beak? Ornithologists (bird scientists) tend to use the term "bill." Some just use "bill" to refer to fleshier beaks (like duck bills). But the two words are basically synonymous, so if a grumpy birder tries to correct you on your word choice, bill them for your time.

Eyes

Pigeon eyes aren't subtle. They're typically a striking orange that fades to yellow near the pupils. This coloration varies, though; some birds have red and white eyes, and some have all-dark eyes. The eyes of young pigeons are a drabber gray or brown.

Like all birds, pigeons are highly visual animals. They need to be able to navigate through the air *and* spot teeny crumbs in sidewalk cracks. They have a huge visual field; like many prey animals, they've got eyes on the sides of their head so they can watch for danger coming from all directions. Your eyes, on the other hand, face forward. That's because your ancestors needed good depth perception, perhaps to climb trees or catch prey. Pigeons do have a bit of binocular vision where their eyes' visual fields overlap at the front of their head. And they can see colors we can't, like ultraviolet. When a pigeon cocks its head and stares at the world, it's seeing more than you could imagine.

Third Eyelids

A pigeon has more eyelids than you. It has three per eye—two opaque eyelids on the top and bottom, plus a third, horizontally closing eyelid called the nictitating membrane. This transparent eyelid cleans and protects the eye but doesn't block vision. Tons of animals have nictitating membranes, including sharks, lizards, beavers, our beloved cats and dogs, and many others. Your animal ancestors had them, too. In fact, take a close look

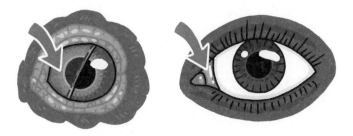

A pigeon's nictitating membrane and your nictitating membrane.

at the corner of your eye: You've still got a fold of tissue (called the plica semilunaris) that's a vestigial nictitating membrane!

Ears

Do pigeons even *have* ears? Yes, but they're usually hidden. While humans possess ostentatiously flappy outer ear bits called pinnae, a pigeon just has holes. Inside a pigeon's ear hole, you'll find the eardrum, cochlea, and all the other internal auditory hardware. The ear hole is usually covered up by a group of special plumes, called auricular feathers, that protect it from the wind yet allow sound to pass through. When pigeons are young and their feathers are sparse, you can see the ear hole as a dark spot behind and below the eye.

Pigeons can hear many things you can't. Deep ocean waves, earthquakes, distant storms, and other perturbations make infrasound—frequencies that are below the limit of human hearing. But pigeons can detect these rumblings. They may use this skill to build up an acoustical map of their world that helps them navigate.

Nostrils and Cere

A pigeon's nostrils aren't as visible as a human's. Called nares (say it like "Aries" with an *n*), they're located near the base of the upper beak. They're difficult to see because they're partly covered by a hard overhanging bit called an operculum and a pale fleshy lump called a cere (say it like "sear"). Nobody's sure why pigeons have a cere. It might protect the nostrils or help with odor detection. Or perhaps it signals something important to prospective mates—male pigeons have slightly bigger ceres than females.

Feathers

A pigeon's feathers, like its beak, are made of keratin, and they're *amazing*. Feathers are tough and flexible enough to withstand the rigors of flight, but they're soft enough to make a warm blanket for pigeon chicks. Most feathers have a stiff central

rachis

barb

barb

barbules

shaft, called a rachis, that branches into thinner bits, called barbs. The barbs split into hooked parts, called barbules. Pigeons use their beaks to zip the barbules on adjacent barbs together so that their feathers stay smooth and sleek for flying. That's partly why they spend so much time preening and making themselves look pretty. They're not vain; they're covered in tiny zippers that need to be zipped.

Iridescent Neck Patch

A pigeon is pretty (seriously, fight me), and its prettiest part is probably the iridescent purple and green neck. This iridescence plays an important role in a pigeon's courtship display and seems to reflect the health of a bird to its potential mates. Amazingly, there isn't a single drop of true purple or green pigment in those feathers. Their hue comes from their structure. A special layer of the feather reflects light. Each neck feather is capable of shining both purple and green, and the color depends on the angle. Some neck feathers look purple when viewed straight on, then turn green when you see them at an angle. Others look green from the front and purple at an angle.

Dust

A pigeon isn't dirty, but it *is* dusty, and that dustiness might contribute to its reputation as a filthy bird. In fact, it's so dusty that if it smacks into a window, it leaves behind a perfectly pigeon-shaped impression of chalky-looking residue. But that dust isn't waste (like the dead skin cells that we humans are constantly dropping). It's a beauty product. Made of keratin particles shed by special feathers, it helps protect feathers and keep them smooth and flexible. When a pigeon preens, it spreads this dust all over its body. Only a singular group of birds, including herons, parrots, storks, and a few others, make this precious cosmetic dust. They all look fantastic, so it must be working.

Wings

A pigeon's wings are basically its front legs. In fact, your arms aren't that anatomically different from bird wings. A pigeon has elbows beneath its feathers. It even has hand bones—though it has fewer of them than you do, and they're shaped differently. The thumb bones attach to a set of stiff feathers,

The alula.

forming a structure called an alula (or, more unfortunately, a bastard wing). The alula improves lift and prevents stalling when a bird is flying slowly or landing. And you thought your opposable thumbs were *so great*.

Tail and Rump

A pigeon's broad, rectangular tail generates lift and helps it brake and balance during flight. For such an important body part, the tail is pretty simple—it's mostly made of feathers. The first birds, like their reptilian ancestors, had long, bony tails instead. In fact, you can see this ancient history play out if you look at a bird embryo; it develops several tail bones that later fuse into a nubbin called a pygostyle. This fused bone is part of the uropygium, the lump at a bird's butt end; it is also unflatteringly known as a pope's nose or parson's nose.

Many pigeons also have a striking white patch on their rump (above the tail). This flashy butt may help them evade one of the world's fastest predators: the peregrine falcon. When a hungry falcon dives at a pigeon—at speeds of up to a whopping 200 miles per hour (322 kph)—the pigeon often rolls to the side to evade it. That white rump may draw the falcon's attention away from the wings so that it fails to anticipate the pigeon's evasive maneuver.

Feet

Shh! Pigeons are sneaking up on you. When they walk, they stand on tiptoe, holding the bones of their legs that correspond to the midfoot bones of a human up off the ground. Birds' ankles are located about halfway up their legs, roughly where you'd expect to see their knees. This gives rise to the persistent myth that birds have backward-pointing knees. Their true knees are nestled up near their belly, usually hidden by feathers and skin.

Compared to the rest of its body, a pigeon's legs look reptilian. They're covered in tiny scales and topped with larger rectangular ones. For a long time, scientists thought that these scales were a sort of throwback to a bird's reptilian ancestors. But new evidence suggests that they may have evolved independently, originating from feathers. Biology will trick you at every available opportunity.

Cloaca

If you flip over a pigeon and look for its genitalia … well, first off, why are you doing this? Second, you won't find anything but a hole. A pigeon's eggs, sperm, and poop all come out through an opening in a special chamber called the cloaca. To reproduce, a pigeon lines up its hole with its lover's hole (probably the worst phrase ever included in a field guide) and they rub them together until the male ejaculates sperm into the female. It's called the "cloacal kiss." You're welcome.

In the bird world, penises are passé. Bird ancestors had penises, but many avian groups independently lost their penises over the course of evolution. Only about 3 percent of bird species today have them. They aren't exactly like mammal penises, either; the urethra isn't a sealed-up tube but an open groove that sperm travels along. Scientists don't know why most birds lost their external genitalia. Maybe it's just easier to fly without dangly bits.

BIRDS THAT HAVE PENISES

Cassowaries	Guans
Chachalacas	Rheas
Curassows	Ostriches
Ducks	Screamers (yes, this is
Emus	a real kind of bird)
Geese	Swans

Parasites

Hey, don't judge. Every critter is susceptible to parasites. Your dog gets them—fleas, heartworms, ticks, and more. You get them—lice, scabies, tapeworms, and the same ticks that chomp on your dog. Even parasites get parasites. We're all just living, breathing habitats for smaller creatures. Pigeons are no exception. Their insides are home to wormlike nematodes, flukes, tapeworms, and single-celled protists like *Trichomonas gallinae* (related to the parasite that causes the human sexually transmitted disease trichomoniasis). These internal tagalongs are called endoparasites. A pigeon's outside is home to ectoparasites like mites, bugs, fleas, flies, ticks, and lice that cling to its feathers and skin and nibble on them.

FEELING LOUSY

Pigeons get lice, just like you and me. And just like us, they can preen away these pesky parasites. But the lice adapt to this onslaught in an astonishing way. A team of biologists at the University of Utah and the University of Illinois put *Columbicola columbae* lice on dark- and light-colored pigeons and left them alone for four years. As the pigeons preened off the lice they could see, the lice evolved, becoming darker on the dark birds and lighter on the light birds.

A Columbicola columbae pigeon louse.

Pigeons have a secret weapon to wield against their external freeloaders. They use their beaks to preen their feathers, and they're quite effective at removing parasites. They'll even pick parasites from each other. They pay special attention to the heads of other pigeons, since it's hard to preen your own head with your own mouth (do not try this).

INSIDE BITS

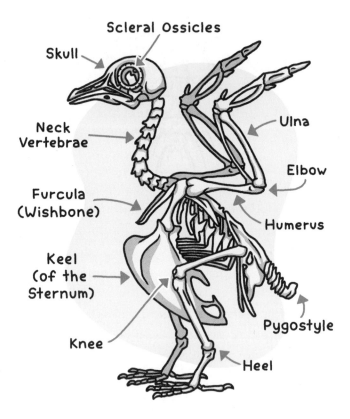

Skull

Scleral Ossicles

Neck
Vertebrae

Furcula
(Wishbone)

Keel
(of the
Sternum)

Knee

Ulna

Elbow

Humerus

Pygostyle

Heel

A pigeon skeleton.

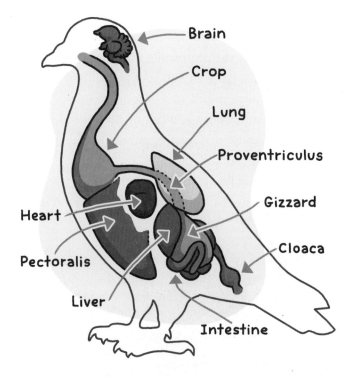

Brain

Crop

Lung

Proventriculus

Gizzard

Cloaca

Heart

Pectoralis

Liver

Intestine

Selected inside bits.

Lungs and Air Sacs

A pigeon breathes more rapidly than you do—twenty-eight times per minute, compared to your twelve to twenty breaths. That's pretty neat, but what's *really* neat is that it breathes in a totally different way.

When you inhale, your diaphragm, a muscle below your lungs, contracts and moves down. Along with some muscles between your ribs, the contracting diaphragm causes your chest to expand, sucking air into your lungs. Then the blood vessels in your lungs grab oxygen from the air and spew waste carbon dioxide into your lungs. When you breathe out, your diaphragm relaxes and you release that carbon dioxide into the air. It's a good system—but don't get cocky. It's not as hyperefficient as it could be. Your lungs don't empty out completely as you exhale, so you always hang on to some stale, oxygen-poor air.

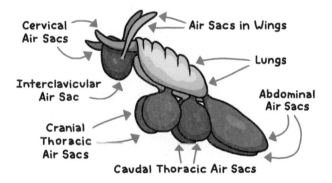

A simplified diagram of pigeon air sacs.

A pigeon, on the other hand, soaks up oxygen even when it's breathing out. It lacks a diaphragm, and its lungs can't expand. Instead, it has nine air sacs whose sole purpose is to push air through the lungs from the back to the front in the most efficient way possible. Air only travels one way through the system. When a bird breathes in, fresh air moves into the lungs and the back air sacs; simultaneously, stale air moves out of the lungs to the front air sacs. When the bird breathes out, stale air moves out of the lungs and front air sacs and fresh air moves from the back air sacs to the lungs. This way, the lungs are constantly bathed in oxygen-rich air. It's a finely tuned system that helps fuel a pigeon's high-octane flying lifestyle.

Bones

There's a stubborn myth about birds. It goes like this: Birds are delicate. They've sacrificed strength and durability so that they're light enough to fly, and their skeletons are fragile and hollow. And sure, it's true that many birds have air-filled pockets in their bones; a pigeon's skeleton is almost totally hollow, with just a few marrow-filled bones (like the radius in the wing and the femur in the leg). But that hollowness isn't weakness. The air pockets act as an extension of a bird's highly efficient respiratory system, and they're crisscrossed with bits of bone to keep the structure strong. The outside of a bird bone is stiff and heavy, so that, on average, a bird's skeleton is even denser than a mammal's.

Bird skeletons have another quality that adds strength and stiffness: Some groups of bones have fused into one. For instance, a pigeon's wishbone, or furcula, is basically your collarbones melded together. All of these adaptations give a pigeon the tough core of strength it needs to withstand the rigors of flight.

Breast Muscles

Have you ever wondered why most of the chicken and turkey meat you'll find in a deli is breast meat? Birds aren't very meaty in general, but they have gigantic breast muscles that power their wings. In pigeons, these muscles may make up nearly a quarter or more of their weight. A pigeon has a large breastbone, or sternum, with a flat part called a keel. (If you're into all things nautical, a keel is also the name for the thick plate that runs along the bottom of a ship.) The muscles that flap a pigeon's wings up and down are all attached to this keel; the bird's back and shoulder muscles are comparatively small. To lower its wings, a pigeon contracts breast muscles called pectorales. To raise its wings, it contracts the smaller supracoracoideus muscles, which pull on tendons attached to the wing bones and tilt them up.

Plexus Venosus Intracutaneous Collaris

Try saying that ten times fast. The plexus venosus intracutaneous collaris is a fascinating feature that deserves your attention—but it's a mouthful. Let's call it the collar plexus for short. This is a dense, complex network of interwoven blood vessels that stretches from a pigeon's head down to an expanding throat pouch called the crop (learn more about the crop on page 82). Pigeons can widen or narrow these vessels, which lets them shed extra heat when they're too hot. Also, a male pigeon has more blood vessels in his collar plexus, which helps him poof up his neck when he's showing off to try to attract some female attention.

Heart

A pigeon may look cold and emotionless, but it has a big heart— at least, a bigger heart in proportion to its body size than yours. That heart tends to beat faster, too. When you're at rest, your ticker thuds 60 to 100 times a minute, whereas a pigeon's beats about 170 times a minute. When you're exercising, your heart rate climbs to 150 to 200 beats per minute (depending on your age), but a flying pigeon's heart rate can skyrocket to an intense 550 beats per minute.

Your heart and a pigeon's have one truly bizarre similarity, though: They both have four hollow regions called chambers (with two atria and two ventricles). This might not seem remarkable, but four-chambered hearts are unusual across the animal kingdom. Fish, for instance, have two-chambered hearts. Amphibians, such as frogs, and reptiles, such as geckos, have three-chambered hearts. But crocodiles and their relatives have four-chambered hearts, as do all mammals and birds. We're part of an elite club. (Starfish have no hearts at all. They're as beautiful as they are uncaring.)

So what's so great about four chambers? Both birds and mammals generate their own body heat to keep themselves warm, which costs a lot of energy and oxygen. A critter with a four-chambered ticker can send a separate stream of blood to the lungs for maximum efficiency. The heart directs oxygen-depleted blood to the lungs so they can reoxygenate it, and it sends a nice, steady flow of oxygen-rich blood to the rest of the body. Otherwise, the oxygen-rich and oxygen-poor blood would mix, producing blood that's just oxygen-meh. Four-chambered hearts are amazing, but here's the *really* amazing thing: Birds and mammals evolved their extra chambers independently, stumbling across the same great idea thanks to the vagaries of evolution.

Blood

Say you're a hard-boiled detective and you're sent to investigate a splash of blood in a dark alley. Can you tell whether the victim was a person or a pigeon? At first glance, it's not easy. Pigeon blood and human blood look similar to the naked eye. But if you take a sample back to the lab and slip it under a microscope, you'll get your answer. A human's red blood cells are round, as are the red blood cells of all mammals, whereas a bird's are oval-shaped. And there's another key difference. Most of your body's cells contain a little DNA-packed ball called the nucleus—the cell's "brain." But human red blood cells squirt out their nucleus, perhaps so they can bend and squeeze more easily through narrow capillaries. Only mammals have evolved these special nucleus-free cells. Birds, however, have DNA-rich red blood cells with a visible nucleus at their center. Case closed, Detective Pigeonlock.

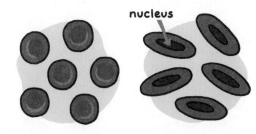

Human red blood cells.   *Pigeon red blood cells.*

Crop and Stomach

A pigeon can't carry a bag to the grocery store, but it has the next best thing: an internal food storage device called a crop. This is an enlarged part of the esophagus, the tube that runs between the throat and the stomach. A pigeon that finds a great source of food can quickly gulp down the goods and store it in its crop for later consumption in a safe location.

Once food passes down a pigeon's esophagus, it enters a peculiar two-part stomach. The first part, the proventriculus, is full of glands that release juices to digest protein. The second part, the ventriculus, is a tough, heavily muscled grinding machine that basically replaces a bird's teeth. The ventriculus is also known as the gizzard—a fun-to-say word that has cropped up (sorry) in a lot of English slang over the centuries. People who worried were once said to be "fretting in their gizzards." A chronically annoying thing was "stuck in your gizzard." Secretly unhappy folks were "grumble gizzards." It's high time we brought the gizzard back into ordinary parlance.

PIGEON MILK

Mooove over, dairy cows. Both male and female pigeons produce a nutritious milk in their crops to feed their babies. You can learn about the wonders and horrors of pigeon milk (hint: it's chunky) on page 179.

Brains and Intelligence

For a long time, people thought that birds were, well, bird-brained. Early scientists noticed that avian brains are relatively smooth and small compared to mammalian brains. They lack a neocortex, a region of the brain that in mammals is the seat of higher functions like cognition and spatial reasoning. Scientists concluded that birds are stupid. But they were wrong.

You can't tell an animal's smarts from its brain size. Bird brains may be teeny compared to ours, but they're relatively large for their body size, and they're thick with neurons. A brain region called the mesopallium has cells similar to those in a neocortex. Bird brains just look different from ours, and that makes sense, since birds and mammals have been evolving on separate paths for hundreds of millions of years.

Some birds are especially brilliant, with brains full of densely packed neural networks. Crows and their relatives, for instance, are cognitive superstars. New Caledonian crows can build tools out of several separate objects. Common ravens are known to drop rocks on researchers who stray too close to their nests.

Parrots are also capable of astonishing mental feats. Alex, a famous African gray parrot who worked with scientist Irene Pepperberg, learned approximately 150 words and could categorize objects by color and shape. Wild parrots are no slouches, either; palm cockatoos craft drumsticks to beat out a tune on a hollow tree, perhaps to impress a mate. "Hey, baby," they seem to be saying, "did you know that I'm a drummer? Okay, so I'm not in a band right now, but I've been going to *a lot* of auditions."

Pigeon brains, however, are not quite as densely packed. This results in some cognitive weak spots. For instance, a pair of pigeons can't recognize their own young until the babies are about ready to fly; you can swap chicks between pigeon nests and the birds won't notice. But scientists have discovered that pigeon brains can accomplish some incredible tasks.

He's not a real doctor.

Here are just a few of the bizarre things these birds have been trained to do:

- Distinguish Impressionist paintings from Cubist paintings

- Tell benign from cancerous human breast tissue (in microscope slides) and diseased heart tissue from nondiseased tissue (in images)

- Remember a set of more than 1,800 separate images with 73 percent accuracy, earning them a solid C grade

- Distinguish Indian dance from martial arts

- Recognize themselves in a video

- Order groups of objects from lowest to highest number

- Learn to distinguish English four-letter words from meaningless combinations of letters

- Play Ping-Pong

DOMESTIC PIGEON BREEDS

The Fanciest Flock

It's time to meet some of the poshest pigeons on the planet. Why take a detour to the land of purebred pigeons? Because you can't separate a pigeon from its past. Every feral bird is the end result of thousands of years of domestication, careful breeding, and then intermixing with whatever other birds flew the coop. If you take some time to learn about domestic breeds, you'll have a better understanding of the patterns and features you'll see in the "wild" birds around you. Plus, purebred pigeons look *amazing*.

HAUTE COO-TURE

Pigeon breeds come in a mind-bending range of shapes, colors, sizes, and even sounds. Some pigeon keepers display their birds at exhibitions—just like dog shows, but with smaller poops. In this section, you'll come face-to-face with a few of the hundreds of breeds.

But first, a word of caution: This is a highly simplified account of an ancient hobby. Some of these breeds come in more than one form. That's because hobbyists must apply a concerted effort to breed birds that excel in a particular characteristic, so they've split bloodlines into separate groups—some for exhibition (looking good at pigeon shows), and others for performance (tumbling through the air or making interesting sounds) or racing (going real fast). The within-breed bloodlines have diverged so much that some can be considered separate breeds.

On to the show!

HOMING PIGEONS

Homing breeds have one job: Get home. They do it with accuracy and speed, carrying messages or winning long-distance races—though a few of them, like the German beauty homer, are now bred for looks instead of skill. Because pigeon keepers often release their homing pigeons into the outdoors for long races, some homers get lost. As a result, a lot of feral pigeon populations in Europe and North America have genes from these wayward birds.

Example: Racing Homer

Origin: The racing homer is the thoroughbred of pigeons. The breed is about 220 years old, and it's a perfect blend of two impressive homing pigeon strains (one from England and one from Belgium). Racing homers are popular worldwide, especially in Asia, where the best racers can fetch more than a million dollars.

The look: Racing homers seem like normal feral pigeons at first, but take a closer look. Note the deep, powerful chests for sustained and rapid flapping. These birds come in a variety of colors and patterns, from opal to smoky to ash, but their appearance isn't important so long as they're swift, adept navigators.

Odd fact: In 1998, a retiring pigeon keeper in Skipton, England, gave a bird named Boomerang to a friend in Algeciras, Spain. Aptly named, Boomerang took off and flew 1,200 miles back home. Next, the keeper gave the bird to a friend in England; ten years later, Boomerang showed up at his door yet again. No power in the world can stop true dove.

OTHER FLYING/SPORTING BREEDS

These birds are bred for their peculiar way of moving. They zoom up high, stay aloft for a long time, tumble through the air, or roll along the ground.

Example: Birmingham Roller

Origin: This breed was developed in Birmingham, England, sometime before the 1870s (nobody's sure when).

The look: The Birmingham roller looks pretty ordinary; it doesn't have fancy feathers, and it comes in a typical mix of pigeon colors and patterns. But when it flies, something bizarre happens: The bird flips over backward, rolling several times through the air.

Odd fact: The Birmingham roller is just one of many breeds that somersault when they fly. It remains unclear why this happens. Different breeds roll in different ways—tumblers somersault once or twice in a row, whereas rollers do it many times. Some types, like parlor rollers, can't fly at all and somersault along the ground.

UTILITY BREEDS

Okay, "utility" is a euphemism. Utility pigeons can't help you fix broken furniture or plumb your toilet. They're bred for one use: meat. They're big, beefy animals that grow up fast. Some of them, however, are now prized for their looks.

Example: American Giant Runt

Origin: People in Italy and Spain have been developing various types of runt pigeons for millennia. The American giant runt is a uniquely American mix of these breeds. It debuted at a pigeon exposition in Philadelphia in 1873.

The look: Perhaps the most hilariously named pigeon, the American giant runt isn't runty at all. Whereas most feral pigeons weigh around 0.75 pound (0.34 kg), an American giant runt can weigh 3 pounds (1.36 kg), about four times more. That's a lot of pigeon. It is powerfully built, with a big head and broad shoulders.

Odd fact: In the first century CE, the Roman writer Pliny the Elder noted that "Many persons have quite a mania for pigeons. . . . It is thought that those of Campania attain the largest size." These chunky Italian birds may have been the forebearers of the runt breeds.

Example: King Pigeon

Origin: This breed comes from the United States. The white king variety, which is probably the world's most popular meat pigeon, was developed in 1890 from a blend of four others: the runt, the homer, the gentle duchess, and the tall, compact Maltese.

The look: Picture a beefcake of a pigeon. A meaty, gym-rat pigeon that drinks protein shakes and asks if you even lift. That's a king pigeon. It won't grow to be as large as the American giant runt, but it'll get close: It can reach almost 2.33 pounds (1 kg).

Odd fact: If you work at an animal shelter, you're probably familiar with king pigeons. They're often found wandering the streets. Well-meaning people buy them from meat markets and release them—but this kind gesture is a death sentence. The king pigeon's gentle disposition and oddly compact, often radiantly white body make it stand out among the feral birds, and it's hopeless at surviving the rigors of city life. If you run across a king pigeon, consider taking it to an animal shelter (read more about this on page 191). They make great pets, FYI, and they won't steal your protein powder.

ORNAMENTAL BREEDS

Ladies and gentlebirds, the pigeon show is about to take an astonishing turn. Pick any feature of a pigeon's appearance—odds are, there's a breed that pushes this characteristic to the extreme, purely for aesthetic purposes.

Example: Scandaroon

Origin: Originally bred in Iraq, the scandaroon was imported to Germany, where breeders shaped it into its current form. It's also known as the Nuremberg Bagdad.

The look: This bird's face droops downward like a melting watch from a Salvador Dalí painting. Its eyes are ringed in red, making it seem perpetually surprised. In his 1898 book *Pigeons and All About Them*, pigeon fancier F. M. Gilbert drops a harsh burn: "I believe I said somewhere in this work that to me all pigeons were beautiful, but I fear I will have to draw the line on the Scandaroon." (This book's author thinks they're pretty, though.)

Odd fact: On its way to Germany from Iraq, the scandaroon passed through the Turkish port of Iskenderun ("Scandaroon"). In 1735, English writer John Moore named the breed after the port.

Example: Crested Fairy Swallow

Origin: This breed was created in the state of Saxony in Germany, and it remains popular among German pigeon keepers.

The look: The crested or Saxon fairy swallow looks like it has wings on its feet. In fact, in a way, they are wings. Scientists have found that in birds with feathered feet, a gene that helps the wings develop has been switched on in the legs, causing them to grow feathers instead of scales. A bird of this particular breed has stubby legs that flare out into huge fans of feathers known as muffs. It also has a couple types of crests (areas of backward-pointing feathers on the head): Its shell crest runs in a shell-like shape from ear to ear, and its mane runs from the rear of the head down the neck.

Example: African Owl

Origin: This breed was developed in Asia and North Africa, though it's so ancient that the specifics are hazy. It's named for its short, thick beak, which looks somewhat like an owl's.

The look: This is a tiny pigeon, just about 8 inches (20 cm) from its chest to the end of its tail. It has fancy frills on its breast, but perhaps its most obvious traits are its ball-round head—those with rounder heads are more prized—and teeny beak.

Odd fact: If you released a flock of African owl pigeons into the wild, they wouldn't be able to establish a new feral population on their own. Their beaks are so short that they can't effectively feed and raise their babies. When pigeon keepers want to breed more African owls, they take the eggs out of the nest and give them to foster parents that have larger beaks.

Example: Jacobin

Origin: Another ancient breed, the Jacobin is so old that nobody knows where or when it was developed (though many people think it comes from India).

The look: A Jacobin is a regal-looking bird with neck plumage like an extravagant feather boa. Its head is always white, which makes it stand out against an often colorful hood. This is another breed that wouldn't last long in the wild. Because of its hood, the Jacobin can't see well, and it has trouble feeding itself. When it's nesting, its owner has to trim away those neck feathers so that it can care for its young.

Odd fact: If you know about the French Revolution, you're probably wondering whether this bird got its name from the group of radical French revolutionaries known as Jacobins. It didn't, but both the pigeon and the revolutionaries are named after the same thing. Jacobin pigeons are so called because their hoodlike crests resemble the hoods worn by medieval Jacobin friars (called Dominican friars elsewhere). The French revolutionaries held their meetings in a Jacobin monastery.

Example: Frillback

Origin: Nobody's sure where this frilly friend came from—perhaps Turkey, but it had reached England by 1765.

The look: The barbs of a frillback's feathers grow unevenly and end up misaligned, causing a curl. The feathers aren't all equally curled; some of the body plumes twist like a pig's tail, but others, like those on the tail and wingtips, are only a little bit rippled, so the frillback is still able to fly. Interestingly, this breed is a good example of the way that pigeon fashion standards change over time. In Darwin's day, frillback feathers were only a little twisted. Today, the breed is dripping with curls.

Odd fact: The frillback isn't the only pigeon with peculiarly shaped feathers. Two mutations called silky and porcupine produce equally dramatic effects. An exhibition fantail pigeon with the silky mutation has feathers whose barbules don't lock together correctly, so they're fluffy. A porcupine pigeon isn't an accepted pigeon variety; it's a rare, accidental mutation that produces spiky plumage due to errors in feather growth. Such a bird is unable to become airborne, much like an actual porcupine.

Example: Fantail

Origin: This breed is at least eight centuries old. Its origins are mysterious, but it may have come from India.

The look: There are a lot of extreme pigeon breeds, but the fantail is one of the extremest. With its knees tucked up against its sides, it stands low, its body almost spherical. Its spectacular fanlike tail makes it look like a tiny Thanksgiving turkey. The fantail's tail isn't just strangely shaped. It's packed with three times more feathers than a wild pigeon's, making it look extra luxuriant.

Odd fact: Fantails aren't usually great at flying. A pigeon keeper who breeds fancy flying birds may keep a white fantail and use it to entice the other birds home to roost. Known as a dropper, this fantail is placed at the entryway to the loft. It's a bright beacon whose presence says, "Hey, there's good food in here!" Enthusiastically, the fancy fliers drop out of the sky to join their pal.

Example: English Pouter

Origin: This particular breed comes from seventeenth-century England, and its ancestors were pouters from the Netherlands.

The look: Picture a tall person who just won an argument and leaps to their feet to puff out their chest with pride. That's an English pouter. This bird has an enormous crop accentuated by its tall, skinny body. Feathery feet complete the striking look.

Odd fact: You can see its knees—and that's unusual. Pigeon knees are usually tucked into the chest fluff. But because the English pouter was bred to have an unusually upright posture, its feathery knees are exposed to the world.

Example: Archangel

Origin: This is another old breed with a mysterious past— a common refrain, since the history of pigeon keeping is so very ancient. It may have first appeared in the Russian city of Arkhangelsk, but nobody's sure.

The look: If your favorite part of a pigeon is its iridescent neck feathers, then the archangel is the breed for you. Its body is a lustrous bronze. Its wing color can vary, but if it has dark wings, they glimmer with a beetle-green sheen. Some archangels also have a little crest or striking white wing feathers that enhance their fancy appearance.

Odd fact: In England, all color forms of this breed other than the one portrayed above are called Gimpels. Why? In Germany, the breed is called Gimpeltaube, after the German name for the Eurasian bullfinch, a beautiful reddish, gray, and black song- bird whose plumage resembles this type of pigeon.

Example: Arabian Trumpeter

Origin: The breed is hundreds of years old, and most likely originated in Saudi Arabia.

The look: The Arabian trumpeter is a dark-eyed, stout bird that comes in many attractive colors . . . blah, blah, blah. You don't need to know what it looks like. You need to hear how it *sounds*. This pigeon was bred for its distinctive voice. Rather than cooing, it makes a remarkable hooting, laughing call, sort of like "Wa ha ha ha ha ha!"

Odd fact: The Arabian trumpeter is just one of many breeds developed for their surprising sounds. Another is the Thai laugher, which has a harsher, more mocking laugh. So, if you want a good audience for your comedy sets, try practicing in front of Arabian trumpeters.

FERAL PLUMAGES AND PATTERNS

Spot Them All

Every pigeon flock is a rainbow—a slightly limited, earth-toned rainbow. When fancy purebred pigeons escape into the wild, they blend their bloodlines to make the birds we see on the streets. Some of their most astonishing characteristics, like feathery hoods that block their vision, fade away. But other traits, like crests or white-blotched wings, persist, making each flock a feast for the eyes. Let's take a look at the genetic origins of these patterns and plumages and raise your pigeon-watching skills to the next level.

A QUICK PRIMER ON GENETICS

Always on the lookout for amazing new variations, pigeon breeders have spent centuries uncovering the formulas for inherited plumage colors and patterns. More recently, genetic scientists have joined in; they love to study pigeons because, by uncovering the sources of various fancy traits, they can learn more about bird evolution as a whole. Scientists and breeders are still unraveling the mysteries of pigeon coloration, so the facts in the next few pages are just pieces of the puzzle—but they're dazzling pieces.

Luckily, you don't need to be a scientist to understand the basics of plumage genetics. You just need to know a few key terms from biology class.

DNA: This long, spiraling molecule contains the blueprints for making a living thing. Almost all the cells in your body have DNA. Those letters stand for deoxyribonucleic acid, which is very fun to say.

PLAY A PIGEON GENETICS COMPUTER GAME

The lab of Dr. Michael Shapiro at the University of Utah informed much of the genetic info in this section. This lab, in collaboration with the Genetic Science Learning Center, developed an online game called Pigeonetics that lets you explore the genetics of pigeon patterns in detail. You can find it at learn.genetics.utah.edu/content/pigeons/pigeonetics.

Gene: A gene is a chunk of DNA that contains a particular set of instructions.

Allele: Like candies or popsicles, genes can come in two or more flavors, and these flavors are called alleles. For example, some people have wet earwax and others have dry earwax. That's because there's an allele for wet earwax and another one for dry. By sticking a finger in your ear, you can learn something about your DNA.

DNA

Dominant: You typically get one allele of a gene from each parent, so you wind up with two. Sometimes both of these alleles have the same flavor. But if you wind up with two different flavors of alleles, a strange thing happens. Certain alleles are pushy and "dominant," preventing other alleles from affecting how you look, act, or function. For example, the allele for wet earwax is dominant over the allele for dry earwax. If you get at least one copy of the wet earwax allele, you always have wet earwax. (Note that dominance is relative; an allele may be dominant to one allele but not to another.)

Recessive: An allele that is dominated by another allele is "recessive" to that allele. The dry earwax allele is recessive to the wet earwax allele.

FROM POPULAR LOOKS
TO UNIQUE STYLES

Plumage colors and patterns aren't evenly mixed among pigeon flocks, and that makes things interesting. Some looks are intriguingly rare. There are a couple of reasons for this. First, certain plumages are genetically recessive to others, like the brick-red look known as "recessive red," so they're just less likely to appear in pigeon chicks. Birds with those plumages are the result of very particular genetic circumstances.

More bizarrely, there's some evidence that birds of certain hues and patterns have a better chance to make it to adulthood. Scientists Daniel Haag-Wackernagel, Philipp Heeb, and Andreas Leiss found that young pigeons in Vienna, Austria, with T-check patterns on their wings had a better chance of growing up, and birds with barred wings were less likely to survive. Why? We don't know. We can't say that those patterns *cause* birds to survive better in urban settings, but pigeons

WHY PIGEON FEATHERS ARE LIKE SUNTANS

A pigeon's body color comes from the amount and arrangement of pigments called melanins. Human skin color also comes from melanins. When a person tans, their body makes more melanin to protect itself from sun damage, turning the skin darker.

with those patterns may be more likely to inherit helpful behavioral or physical qualities. For instance, darker birds seem to breed more readily throughout the year than lighter birds.

LOCAL PIGEON PRIDE

Up until now, we've been talking as if all the world's feral pigeons are one cohesive type of bird—but that's not really the case. Each group of ferals has its own history. Those in Cairo, for example, originated from escaped Middle Eastern birds, and they've been feral for longer than humans have been keeping written historical records. But ferals in New York City come from pigeons brought to North America just four centuries ago.

Even among birds who live in the same general area, geography splits them into separate groups. Researchers Elizabeth Carlen and Jason Munshi-South found a genetic gap between the pigeons of Providence, Rhode Island, and nearby New Haven, Connecticut. Pigeons from urban Providence and cities north, like Boston, just don't make the hop across the suburbs of Connecticut to pahk their cahs in the yahds of New York City birds.

Different environments pose different challenges, seeming to favor birds of particular colors and patterns. For instance, birds with the blue bar pattern are more common in rural areas and at lower latitudes. Darker-colored birds (with patterns like T-check and check) are more likely to be found in cities and at higher latitudes. Scientists aren't sure why, but again, they think that birds with particular plumages might have behaviors or physiologies that keep them alive in those circumstances—perhaps stemming from genetic mixing between feral pigeons and their closely related cousins, the speckled pigeons (see page 211). These differences manifest in strange ways. After the Chernobyl nuclear disaster, blue bar pigeons were more susceptible to illness, and they declined in number more than other pigeon types. (Please don't re-create that experiment at your local park.)

THE Zs AND Ws OF
PIGEON CHROMOSOMES

Oddly, a female bird always gets her base color from her dad. Here's why. Genes are packaged into paired units called chromosomes. In humans, the most well-known pair is made up of the sex chromosomes, named for their shape: X and Y. But birds, just to be confusing, have Z and W sex chromosomes. Male birds have ZZ and females have ZW. The gene for a pigeon's base body color is only found on the Z chromosome, so females only get one copy of it, and it comes from Dad.

BASE COLOR

Now that you know the basics, let's take a closer look at pigeon plumages. We'll start with the bird's base color, meaning its main plumage color. A single gene controls this hue, and it comes in three flavors: ash-red, blue, or brown. Here's a diagram that shows the relative genetic dominance of these three main colors:

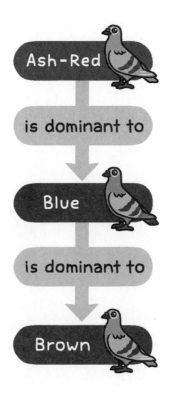

Ash-Red

What to spot: An ash-red bird has a gray and cinnamon-hued body. If it has wing markings, they're red. It lacks a dark tail tip. You'll see this hue less often than blue but more often than brown.

The genetics: The allele for ash-red body color is dominant over the other two colors. So, a bird that gets at least one ash-red allele from a parent will always be ash-red.

Blue

What to spot: A blue bird is mostly a stormy blue-gray, and it usually has gray-black markings on its wings and a dark bar on its tail. This color is closest to the plumage of a feral pigeon's wild ancestors. When you spot a blue bird, imagine it in the time before domestication, perched at the edge of a lonely cliff, the wind ruffling its feathers.

The genetics: The allele for blue body color is dominant to the brown one, so a pigeon who gets one brown and one blue allele will be blue. It's recessive to the ash-red one. Even though ash-red is dominant, blue body color is the most common hue in feral pigeons, meaning that there's something about blue birds that makes them more able to survive in the wild. We don't know what that is!

Brown

What to spot: A brown bird is usually gray-brown with chocolate markings. This is the rarest body color of the three, so if you see a brown pigeon, consider yourself blessed by the pigeon gods. (To learn which ancient gods are tied to pigeons and thus require your devotion, see page 35.)

The genetics: The alleles for all the other colors are dominant over the brown allele. In order to be brown, a bird can't inherit alleles for any other color.

A RAINBOW OF PLUMAGE POSSIBILITIES

The three base colors we just covered are important to pigeon coloration, but if they were the be-all and end-all, pigeon breeding would get pretty boring. Other factors can affect pigeon body color, producing plumages like spread, recessive red, recessive white, piebald, and dilute. Here are some of those factors and the science behind them. (There are many others beyond this list, too, with evocative names like dirty, grizzle, almond, sooty, smoky, and opal.)

Spread

What to spot: Have you ever seen a pigeon without any sort of fancy wing or tail pattern, one that looks like it took a bath in a single color of paint? That's called spread. The spread gene changes the way the three basic body colors—ash-red, blue, and brown—play out, erasing most of the subtlety and "spreading" one color all over. This is usually a less common mutation, and it's a cool one to see.

Spread ash-red: This bird is a pale, red-tinged gray all over.

Spread blue: This bird is blue-black all over.

Spread brown: This bird is brown all over.

Spread Ash-Red

Spread Blue

Spread Brown

The genetics: This characteristic comes from a single gene that modifies the body color. There are two kinds of alleles for the gene: spread and not-spread. The spread allele is dominant over the not-spread one, so a bird with just one spread allele will have this pattern.

Recessive Red

What to spot: Like spread birds, a recessive red bird is patternless; it's brick red all over, with a pale beak. But this plumage is caused by its own genetic mutation. If you find a recessive red bird, you should feel proud of yourself—you've discovered a rarity!

The genetics: This look is caused by a single gene. It has two alleles: a recessive allele that makes a bird red, and a dominant one that makes a bird not-red. In order to be recessive red, a pigeon needs two copies of the recessive allele.

Recessive White

What to spot: A recessive white bird looks the most like an iconic dove of peace. It has all-white plumage, pinkish claws, and a pinkish beak. The eyes aren't orange and red like most pigeons; they're all-dark. This bird stands out like a bright star against the darker hues of the flock.

The genetics: Recessive white is just one kind of all-white plumage; there are many. But recessive white birds always have dark eyes. That's because their irises lack the typical pigments, so the dark pigments at the back of the eye are visible; pigeon keepers call this a "bull" eye. Though recessive white birds are totally white, they aren't albino. You aren't likely to see true albino pigeons outside of a pigeon breeder's loft. They have poor eyesight that makes it hard for them to survive in the wild.

Piebald (White Patches)

What to spot: Many pigeons have splotches of white on their heads, wings, and other body parts that erase patches of their basic body color. You may see pigeons with just a little spot of white, or birds that are mostly white with only limited patches of color showing through.

The genetics: It's complicated. Many possible mutations can cause white patches, some recessive and some dominant, and different mutations cause white spots on different parts of a pigeon's body.

Dilute

What to spot: A dilute pigeon looks like a regular pigeon with washed-out (or diluted) colors and patterns. Think of a poster that has faded in the sun or a worn-out pair of jeans.

The genetics: One gene determines whether a bird looks diluted. It comes in a bunch of different alleles, and some of them dilute the body color more than others.

*Dilute
Blue Bar*

*Dilute
Recessive Red*

*Dilute
Spread Blue*

Juvenile Pigeons

What to spot: Like young humans, young pigeons have their own style. Since a juvenile pigeon isn't ready to compete for mates, its color pattern is often drab. It may have gray-brown plumage (though this varies from bird to bird) and little to no iridescence on its neck. Whereas an adult pigeon has striking red-orange eyes, a juvenile's eyes are gray, brown, or yellow. Its cere (the swelling above its nostrils) is the same color as its beak, and it's relatively small, which makes the beak look big and awkward—but, arguably, pretty cute. A young pigeon will molt (see page 155) into its adult plumage when it's about fifty days old or so.

WING PATTERNS

Now that you've mastered the basics of pigeon body color, let's zoom in on another characteristic that defines their unique style: wing pattern. The patterns on a pigeon's wings fall into four categories: T-check, check, bar, and barless. These patterns are dictated by a single gene that comes in four alleles, and you can see their relative dominance in the chart below.

Here's something amazing about pigeon wing patterns: Some of them may have originated in a cross-species romance. There's a beautiful African bird called the speckled pigeon (learn more about it on page 211) that's closely related to our pigeon; in fact, it's in the same genus, *Columba* (in this case, it's *Columba guinea*). The speckled pigeon is silver-gray and maroon, and its wings have little white T-shaped marks at the tips of the feathers. At some point a few hundred years ago, the speckled pigeon and our pigeon likely interbred, and pigeons subsequently picked up the ability to grow checkered wings.

T-Check

is dominant to

Check

is dominant to

Bar

is dominant to

Barless

T-Check

What to spot: A T-check wing is heavily marked with dark pigment, so that it's almost all gray-black. If you look closely, you'll see small, T-shaped lighter areas at the tips of the feathers. For reasons that scientists don't totally understand, birds with a T-check or check wing pattern do better in urban environments than birds with a bar pattern.

The genetics: The allele for T-check is dominant to the other three patterns, so a bird with at least one T-check allele will have T-check wings.

Check

What to spot: A checkered wing is covered with distinct dark speckles. They don't run together as much as the patches on a T-check wing, and the check pattern looks overall less dark than the T-check pattern.

The genetics: The check allele is dominant to the bar and barless alleles, but recessive to the T-check allele.

Bar

What to spot: A pigeon with bar-patterned wings hearkens back to the original wing pattern of its wild ancestors. This is the original look—some things never go out of style. The wing has only two dark bars (and no other spots).

The genetics: The bar pattern is dominant to the barless allele, but recessive to the check and T-check alleles.

Barless

What to spot: The wing is completely plain, with no bars or checks.

The genetics: This is by far the rarest wing pattern. In fact, you're very, very unlikely to see it in the wild. Why? First off, it's genetically unlikely. The barless allele is recessive to all of the other patterns, so only birds that get one barless allele from each parent will be barless. Second, it can be linked with vision problems, making it a hindrance to pigeon survival.

OTHER WEIRD DOMESTIC TRAITS TO LOOK FOR

Every now and then you'll see a bird with rare, special traits that go beyond pattern or color, such as unusual feather growth or multicolored toenails. Here are some intriguing purebred traits that still pop up in feral birds.

Head Crest

What to spot: Sometimes you'll find a feral pigeon that has a small tuft of feathers sticking up from the back of its head like a cowlick. It's showing off a unique quality that thrills pigeon fans.

The origin: A crested bird has a mutation that makes its neck feathers grow up toward its head instead of down toward its tail. This characteristic evolved just once in all of pigeon history, from a single gene's mutation. Pigeon breeders used this magical mutant to make a whole host of crested breeds, from Hungarian giant house pigeons to Transylvania double-crested tumblers. Just one gene determines whether a bird has a crest, but many "modifier" genes can shape the crest into a variety of cranial decorations, from tiny peaks to elegant hoods.

Larger Eye Rings

What to spot: All pigeons have rings of skin around their eyes, but some feral pigeons have bigger, fleshier rings.

The origin: By selecting birds with slightly larger eye rings, pigeon keepers enhanced the trait until they developed breeds with giant pink doughnuts of skin around their eyes. You won't see ferals with huge eye doughnuts, but you'll sometimes find birds with fleshier rings.

Feathered Feet

What to spot: Some feral pigeons have feathery legs and feet. The amount of feathering can vary from a few sparse tufts to a ton of fluff that drags on the ground and gets dirty. Ah, the price of fashion.

The origin: Genetically speaking, those foot feathers are basically little wings. In birds with foot feathers, a gene for wing development is being expressed in the feet.

Multihued Toenails

What to spot: Pigeons can have dark toenails, white toenails, or a mix.

The origin: The wild ancestors of feral pigeons had gray-black nails. But as pigeon keepers changed and enhanced the feather colors of their birds, they also changed their toenail colors. White-plumed king pigeons, for example, have all-white toes to match.

Fancy Eye Colors

What to spot: Most pigeon eyes are orange-red, but some have unusual hues such as dark brown or pearly white.

The origin: Orange-red eyes are the original wild form, and the color comes from pigments and blood vessels. Dark-eyed birds lack pigments (read about this on page 115). Birds with white eyes lack an orange-yellow pigment. But that's just the basics of pigeon eye color; it's an eye-wateringly complex subject.

DECODING PIGEON BEHAVIOR

Why Is That Pigeon Doing That Thing?

heyyyy

If you watch a pigeon throughout the day, you'll see it do so much more than peck for food and crap on statues. It may dance, chase another bird, clap its wings, kiss its mate, take off almost vertically, or feed milk to its young. A pigeon is living the complex, nuanced life of a modern-day dinosaur. Here are some of the behaviors you'll see.

HOW TO SPEAK PIGEON

Pigeons are famous for their cooing, but why do they do it? And how else do they communicate with their pigeon pals? Read on to uncover their full repertoire, from coos and grunts to claps and whistles.

Display Coo

What you'll hear: A deep, partly trilled cooing sound that rises and then falls.

Why it happens: The display coo is all about showing off.

coo-ROOK-cťoo-coo

Even if you don't know a ton about pigeons and doves, you probably know that they coo. And it really does sound like *coo*—the word "coo" is onomatopoeic. Note that not all members of the pigeon family make this sound; many do, but some produce weird quacks, chatters, and other noises. The orange dove, for example, sounds like a ticking metronome (see page 18).

If you watch a pigeon coo, you'll notice something weird. Whereas many songbirds open their beaks wide when they belt out a tune, a pigeon's mouth stays shut the whole time. When a dove or pigeon coos, air passes through the syrinx (a vocal organ at the base of the windpipe) and builds up in that poofy expanding crop.

The display coo is a male pigeon's song, though you'll sometimes hear it from female pigeons, too. When a male is ready to mate, he makes this sound during the bow-coo display (see Singing and Dancing on page 162). Part of the song is a trill and part of it is more of an *oo* sound, though the particulars can vary. While display cooing, the male bows and spreads his tail, strutting around his potential mate. But he's not just interested in wooing a female. He also wants to intimidate other males who might be hanging out nearby.

Advertising Coo

What you'll hear: A moaning *ooh-ooh-ooh* sound.

Why it happens: You'll hear this call when a pigeon is looking for love, or when a pair is strengthening their bond at their nesting site.

If you've ever had pigeons nesting outside your apartment window, you know the advertising coo. It's a really weird noise. Lacking the gentle trill of the display coo, it sounds oddly human, like a deep-voiced person going "Woo! WOO!"

Male pigeons make advertising coos when they're ready to start a relationship. They hang out on a perch near a possible nest site and coo away until a female pigeon drops by to visit. Later, both males and females make this coo at the nesting spot. This may help reinforce their bond or encourage the male to go gather some twigs for the nest. The pair will complement the calls with a fetching display of head bobbing and delicate wing twitching.

Food Call

What you'll hear: A baby pigeon making a wheezy whistle.

Why it happens: The chick is encouraging its parents to bring it some food.

FWEEEEEEP
FWEEEEEEP
FWEEEEEEP
FWEEEEEEP
FWEEEEEEP

Odds are, you've heard this call without realizing it. Pigeon chicks can't produce the deep-throated coos of adult birds until they're seven to eight weeks old; instead, they make whistling, wheezing, high-pitched peeps. Once you start noticing these calls, you'll find that there are hidden pigeon nests everywhere.

By crying out, a baby pigeon is saying, "Hey! I'm a baby, and I'm *hungry*! Gimme that milk!" The chick will often pair its call with urgent wing flaps. When it leaves the nest four to six weeks later, it'll still whistle for a while to demand food or signal that it's not a threat to nearby adults.

Wing Clap

What you'll hear: A loud slapping sound as a pigeon takes off.

Why it happens: It's either a way to say "I just had sex" or an expression of alarm.

If you live in a city center, you've probably heard the clapping of startled pigeon wings echoing through the urban canyons. Pigeons make that sound on purpose. On the upswing of a flap, they slap the muscles and stiff feathers of their wingtips together. It's sort of like holding your arms above your head and clapping with your palms turned away from each other.

Pigeons may clap when something startles them into flight, perhaps to warn other pigeons of danger or to scare an approaching predator. But there's another big reason why pigeons make this sound: Males do it as part of a post-sex showoff display (see page 166). It's almost as if they're applauding their own performance. We all know that guy.

Wing Whistle

What you'll hear: A high-pitched whistling sound as a pigeon flies away.

Why it happens: This whistle may help warn other pigeons of approaching danger.

If you startle a pigeon, you'll hear a wheezy whistle as it flaps away. This isn't because its wings are sloppily constructed or because it's panting heavily with the exertion. The whistle is a signal that conveys valuable intel to other pigeons.

When researchers took a close look at the wingtip plumes of pigeons, they discovered a specialized region that's less stiff and flutters in the wind. Was it the source of the whistle? To find out, scientists Robert Niese and Bret Tobalske came up with an ingenious strategy: They grabbed a can of hairspray and applied it to that feather region to stiffen it. Did this dampen the whistle sound? It sure did! Though the whistly wingtip design may come at an aerodynamic cost, it likely helps a pigeon alert its pals of a threat.

To explore this idea, researchers tried recording the wing-whistling sounds of another type of pigeon, the crested pigeon (see page 211 to read more about this bird). When they played the sounds back to the pigeons, the birds burst into the air—the whistle served as a warning. This is what it sounds like when doves fly.

Other Sounds

Pigeons make a few other noises, including:

- **Alarm grunt:** If a potential predator (or scary human) approaches a pigeon, it'll utter a quick grunt. It may also whack the predator with its wings.

- **Stomping feet:** A pigeon may intentionally stomp its feet when it lands, possibly to express its annoyance.

- **Hissing and beak snapping:** When danger threatens the nest, baby pigeons hiss and snap their beaks to try to scare away the intruder.

BASIC BODILY FUNCTIONS

When you're a pampered bird in a dovecote, self-care is easy. Food is free and plentiful, there's lots of clean water, and no predators will disturb your slumber. But how do feral birds take care of themselves? Behold the secrets of pigeon self-maintenance.

Eating

What you'll see: A pigeon strutting along, often as part of a flock, pecking for grain.

Why it happens: Pigeons don't tend to forage in trees; their favorite foods are found on the ground.

TARGET ACQUIRED

Look, just because pigeons eat trash doesn't mean they lack taste. Given the choice, they prefer a mix of protein-rich legumes and grains, including peas, wheat, oats, and corn. In more rural areas, they forage in fields for seeds or visit grain elevators to eat spilled food. In cities, they eat dropped food and weed seeds. They nibble waste from bakeries and visit breweries to feast on spilled barley. They even scarf down insects and other invertebrates. Pigeons aren't huge eaters; all told, they may consume 1 to 2.5 ounces (30 to 70 g) of food per day or so.

Because they're flexible in terms of where, when, and how they look for food, they're better able to survive in places where the seasons change dramatically. This trait also helps them survive us. Human behavior is unpredictable; sometimes we casually drop hot dog buns as if we were benevolent pigeon gods, but other times we chase and harass birds just for the heck of it. We may close down a brewery in one part of the city and reopen it in another, moving the source of tasty grains for reasons that mystify our bird neighbors. Fortunately, pigeons can adapt to our whims.

Drinking

What you'll see: A pigeon dipping its beak into water and slurping it up without tipping its head back to swallow.

Why it happens: Pigeons have a special way of drinking—they're basically living straws.

sluuuurp

Most birds drink by dipping their lower beak into water and then leaning their head back to let the liquid run down their throat. But you won't see a pigeon doing this. Instead, it uses suction. Through delicate movements, it creates areas of low pressure in its mouth and gullet that help it slurp up the water without tossing back its head.

In order to find enough to drink, urban pigeons get creative. They sip from ponds, puddles, rivers, decorative fountains, leaky pipes, pools of water from AC units, and dog bowls placed outside. They even slurp the water from swimming pools—they're especially drawn to the shallow spillway between a hot tub and a pool. And they've learned that water comes from drinking fountains. One bird in Manhattan figured out that it could wait patiently at a fountain for passersby to come and turn it on. Bemused commuters found themselves compelled to push the button for the bird.

Sleeping

What you'll see: A pigeon perched high up on a building, standing on one leg, puffed into a ball.

Why it happens: Pigeons sleep out in the open, not in their nests.

Cartoons lied to us. They told us that nests are basically avian houses, and that all birds settle down to sleep there. But real birds only hang out in nests when they've got eggs or chicks. When they're not raising young, pigeons usually sleep on flat, sheltered surfaces like balconies, eaves, and the roofs of underpasses. They strongly prefer to rest high up so they can avoid hungry mammals that stalk the ground. Researchers have found that when pigeons are prevented from sleeping in a high place, they wake up less rested. Luckily, they have a special trick for staying alert for signs of danger. They can let half of their brain sleep while the other side remains partially awake, keeping the eye on the alert side open to look around.

Here's another cool trick: A pigeon will stand on one leg as it sleeps, while tucking its other leg up into its feathers. Scientists aren't totally sure why they do this. It might help reduce heat loss or give the tucked foot a rest.

Do pigeons dream? When humans sleep, we experience periods of deep, dreamless sleep and chunks of dream-filled sleep characterized by rapid eye movement (REM). Birds do this, too. In fact, of all the animals on Earth, only birds and mammals are known to experience REM sleep. But scientists aren't sure whether birds dream. Some research suggests that songbirds practice their songs in their sleep. When zebra finches sleep, their brain patterns are similar to those in the brains of birds that are awake and singing. Zebra finches even vibrate their vocal cords while they snooze, lending credence to the idea that they're rehearsing. Maybe pigeons dream about cooing.

Power Napping

What you'll see: A pigeon napping, usually in the late afternoon.

Why it happens: Naps help pigeons stay rested—otherwise they need to sleep more deeply at night.

As the day begins to wane, pigeons often take a nap. There's no obvious way to tell a napping pigeon from a sleeping pigeon; they look and act the same. But the location and time of day are key. In the daylight hours, a pigeon is comfortable napping on the ground, near where it may be foraging. At night, it prefers to sleep high up. That's probably because hungry mammals like foxes and coyotes are out hunting in the darkness, looking to snatch a tasty critter off the ground.

For a pigeon, napping isn't just a calming break from pecking at the pavement—it serves an important purpose. If a scary predator or an alarming noise prevents a pigeon from napping, it must make up for that lost rest later. In one study, scientists Dolores Martinez-Gonzalez, John A. Lesku, and Niels C. Rattenborg gently pestered pigeons to keep them from napping. The birds compensated by sleeping more deeply at night. Amazingly, we humans use the same technique. When something cuts into our sleep time on a short-term basis, we catch up by sleeping more deeply later.

Pooping

What you'll see: A pigeon dropping small, round, brown-and-white blobs of waste.

Why it happens: Everybody poops. Pigeons do too, but they don't pee, exactly. Instead, they poop out two kinds of waste at the same time.

wasn't me

We humans poop to get rid of waste left over from digestion (and to spend some quality time on our phones). We also pee, which helps us dispose of extra water and eliminates waste from our bloodstream. So what about birds? They definitely poop—you've probably been the unwelcome recipient of a birdy gift from above—but they don't have bladders, and they don't pee in the same sense that we do.

Both humans and birds make ammonia as a by-product of breaking down proteins. This ammonia is toxic stuff, and bodies need to get rid of it as fast as possible. We humans turn it into a less toxic substance called urea. Then we dilute it with water and pee it out. Birds, on the other hand, convert that waste into uric acid. Though uric acid takes more energy to produce, it's even less toxic than urea, so it doesn't need to be diluted with as much water. It also weighs less, which is useful for flying. Next, bacteria in a bird's guts converts uric acid into other substances, some of which haven't yet been identified— bird waste is rich in secrets. Whatever it's made of, this white stuff comes out of that nifty all-purpose chamber, the cloaca, at the same time as brownish poop. That's why pigeon poop looks like a mix of chocolate and vanilla. Yum!

Some people consider it lucky to get pooped on by a pigeon. If you want to maximize your luck, note that birds often "lighten their loads" right when they take off. (In fact, this author was once totally coated in feces by a pigeon exiting its roost. Years later, a hapless publisher paid her actual money to write about pigeon poop, which is one kind of luck.)

Keeping Cool

What you'll see: A pigeon panting with its beak open, holding its wings away from its body.

Why it happens: When it's hot outside, pigeons can overheat and get sick. But they've got a few smart, unexpected strategies for staying cool.

flutter
flutter

Like dogs, pigeons pant. Their mouths, throats, and respiratory tracts are moist, and panting helps them shed heat through evaporation. Thanks to their amazingly weird respiratory systems, pigeons can pant *and* breathe deeply at the same time. They encourage air flow by waggling their neck muscles in a behavior called gular fluttering. Try this yourself. (It won't work, but it will look hilarious.)

Hot pigeons also hold their wings away from their body, sort of like a sweaty person airing out their pits. Birds don't sweat, exactly, but they do lose water through their skin, which helps them stay cool. They even shed heat through their bare legs and the collar plexus, that complex tangle of veins in their neck. Pigeons that have acclimated to a hot climate and are well hydrated can stay cool even when temperatures soar to 140°F (60°C), and they thrive in super-hot cities like Mecca, Phoenix, and Lagos.

Keeping Warm

What you'll see: A puffed-up pigeon resting in a sunny spot.

Why it happens: Pigeons have some clever tricks for staying toasty when the mercury falls.

In cold weather, we pull on jackets lined with down or artificial fiber—but pigeons have us beat, because they're wearing down-filled jackets all the time. Feathers are great insulators, and cold pigeons will puff up their plumes to trap a layer of warm air around their bodies. They also hang out in sunnier spots on frigid days, clustering on south-facing ledges or roofs to soak up some precious warmth. They shiver, too, which makes their muscles generate heat. And their circulatory system responds to cold temperatures, sending less blood to the skin and to exposed areas like the feet.

Thanks to all of these strategies, pigeons have widened their global domination to include frigid cities like Winnipeg, Anchorage, and Moscow.

GETTING AROUND

Pigeons are deft-enough travelers to make any commuter jealous. Some of them even ride the subway. Here's how pigeons perambulate.

Walking and Running

What you'll see: A pigeon walking across the pavement out in the open.

Why it happens: Many songbirds hop around in dense foliage. But pigeons prefer to strut across the ground.

One of the reasons that people hate pigeons is that these birds tend to hang out on the ground with all the dirt and trash. Pigeons evolved to live out in the open, not in dense, twiggy forests. They eat a lot of fallen grain and seeds, and they typically search for food by walking around and pecking at the ground. If you startle a pigeon, it'll only fly if it absolutely has to, because lifting off costs so much energy. It may just try to run out of your way instead.

Other birds, like the tiny house sparrows you'll find all over cities and suburbs, are hoppers instead of walkers. They spring from twig to twig or bounce across the ground. Nobody's sure why some birds hop and others walk. Sparrows have slender feet that wrap around tree branches; perhaps their leg anatomy, plus their itty-bitty size, make hopping the most efficient means of locomotion for them. But pigeons are hefty, with flat, meaty feet made for moseying.

Head Bobbing

What you'll see: A pigeon bopping its head back and forth as it walks.

Why it happens: The bobbing is an illusion. That pigeon isn't actually bobbing its head back and forth—it's doing something weirder.

vooop

For humans and pigeons alike, it's tough to walk and look at stuff at the same time. We need to gather vital sensory information while also making sure that we don't bump into a neighbor or step in dog poop. Human brains handle this challenge by moving our eyes in precise ways that integrate with the motion of our bodies. We always gaze two steps ahead, and we make imperceptibly quick eye movements as we look from spot to spot.

A pigeon can move its eyes a little, but it also has something we lack: a long, flexible neck. A pigeon neck has twice as many bones as a human's (fourteen, compared to our seven). For a pigeon, the most efficient way to keep tabs on its environment is to shoot its head forward at lightning speed, fix its gaze on something, and keep its head locked in place while its body catches up. So, a pigeon isn't really bobbing its head back and forth; it just looks like it's bobbing because the head moves forward and then the body moves forward to meet it. Clever girl.

Taking Flight

What you'll see: A pigeon taking off by rising almost vertically or dropping down off a perch.

Why it happens: Sometimes pigeons need to make a quick getaway, and they've absolutely mastered the takeoff.

Military engineers have spent decades trying to develop aircraft that can lift off vertically from tight spaces. Joke's on you, military engineers: Pigeons are already there. A pigeon can use its legs to launch nearly vertically into the sky, beating its wings horizontally at a furious eight to nine times per second and generating lift on both the upstroke and the downstroke. This kind of flight uses up a ton of energy, but if it saves the bird from a hungry predator, it's worth it. Some shorebirds and ducks use the same strategy to escape predators; maybe that's because they also serve as prey for the world's fastest animal, the peregrine falcon.

If near-vertical takeoff isn't an option, a pigeon may dive instead, using gravity to its advantage. It springs from its perch on a high ledge and dives straight down. By the time it levels out near the ground, it's zooming along at a speed of 37 miles per hour (60 kph). That's faster than Usain Bolt can run.

Flying

What you'll see: A pigeon powering through the sky or swooping deftly between buildings.

Why it happens: Flight enables a pigeon to search for food in new locations while avoiding ground-based obstacles like cars and hungry mammals—but this ability comes at a substantial cost.

A dove on the wing is the ultimate symbol of freedom. But why do pigeons—and, for that matter, most birds—fly? Many predators are earthbound, including cats, coyotes, and weasels, so the sky is a handy escape route. Plus, a pigeon on the wing has a bird's-eye view of potential food sources, and it can travel swiftly and directly between known foraging spots. Imagine bypassing traffic and taking a private jet straight to your favorite restaurant.

Though flying may *look* effortless, it's subtly difficult. Of all the ways that animals move, powered flight is the most physically demanding. A flying bird expends about ten times more energy than a resting one. And flight is more than just energy-intensive—it's technically challenging.

If you somehow magically grew wings, leapt off a cliff, and started flapping, you would probably say hello to the bottom of the cliff pretty quickly. There's much more to flying than flapping. As a pigeon hurtles through the sky, it makes constant adjustments to maximize lift, minimize drag, swerve around obstacles, and more. When it flies slowly, for example, it tucks its wings on the upstroke, rotating its wingtips backward. At faster speeds, it keeps its wings partially extended. Scientists are still unraveling the complex forces generated by these different configurations, but one thing is clear: Birds aren't just winging it.

Riding the Subway

What you'll see: A pigeon riding a subway car like it thinks it's people.

Why it happens: Pigeons hang out wherever people drop food—and that includes our transit systems.

Pigeons wander San Francisco's BART trains. They forage in the New York City Subway. They flock to the Stockholm Metro and strut onto Toronto's TTC cars. Subway-riding pigeons are everywhere. But here's the million-dollar question: When a pigeon hops on a subway car, does it know where it's going? Probably not. To a pigeon, a subway car is a warm box full of sleepy humans and spilled food. That's about it. Once the bird struts out of the car a few stops later, it doesn't turn around and ride the rails back the way it came. It finds its way out of the station and flies home the old-fashioned way. Maybe we could help by posting tiny subway maps at pigeon eye level—just something to consider.

You've probably shared a train car with a commuting pigeon without even knowing it. They tend to be so quiet and polite that most people don't notice they're there, which is more than you can say for a lot of human commuters.

STAYING PRETTY

Pigeons have a reputation for being dirty, but they're not. In fact, they're beyond fastidious. Pigeons adhere to a rigorous beauty regimen that includes bathing, grooming, and soaking up the sun. All this fuss helps them attract equally handsome mates and keep their feathers in perfect flying condition.

Preening

What you'll see: A pigeon using its beak to carefully clean and arrange its feathers.

Why it happens: Feathers are useful—but they're finicky and need constant care.

A thick coat of feathers is high maintenance. Any sort of disturbance can pull apart the interlocking barbs between feathers and create gaps, and preening helps zip these gaps shut. Luckily, beaks are excellent combs. Pigeons regularly run their beaks through their plumage to keep everything in good flying order.

Feathers also need special care as they grow. Old feathers fall out and must be brushed away. New feathers need particular attention; they develop inside waxy tubes called sheaths that eventually dry and crumble. Preening helps free feathers from their sheaths and remove the resulting debris.

There's another important reason to preen: Parasites love to burrow deep into a warm coat of feathers. Pigeons are great at preening away these unwanted guests, and birds with more parasites will do more preening. Since female pigeons are more likely to choose mates whose plumage looks pristine, preening isn't just about feeling comfortable. It's also about finding love.

Bathing

What you'll see: A pigeon fluttering its wings while standing in water.

Why it happens: Regular baths help pigeons stay healthy and clean.

Next time a friend says, "Eww, pigeons are so dirty," explain that pigeons love baths. They readily wade into puddles, ponds, public fountains, and other shallow water sources. They even take advantage of passing rainstorms ("I'm preeeeeenin' in the rain . . .").

Once they're in the water, pigeons don't settle down for a relaxing soak. Their baths are fast, efficient, and messy. They flap their wings to splash water over their bodies, flaring out their tails and puffing out their plumage so that the water flows between their feathers. They crouch down to vigorously dunk their heads. They even stretch out their wings to give their armpits a good rinse. A bathing pigeon shimmies and shakes, splashing water until it's soaked. Once its bath is finished, everything around it is soaked, too. Never go to a spa with a pigeon.

So long as the bathwater's clean and unpolluted, bathing helps clear dirt from feathers. It might even drown and wash away harmful parasites. A well-washed bird is a happy bird, which is why pet pigeon caregivers provide their charges with ample bathing opportunities.

Sunning

What you'll see: A pigeon lying on the ground, its wings and tail spread wide, looking zoned out.

Why it happens: Don't worry—that pigeon isn't sick. It's catching some rays.

If you're a person who loves birds, it can be upsetting to come across a sunning bird sprawled out motionless, limbs sticking out in various directions. But that bird isn't sick or injured; it's sunning itself, and it's blissfully happy. All sorts of avians, from jays to sparrows to robins to pigeons, love to sun themselves. Scientists are not totally sure why they do it. Maybe it helps heat them up on a cold day. On a hotter day, it may warm and spread the natural oils that keep feathers in top condition. It could help dry a bird's feathers after a bath or cook feather parasites to death. Perhaps it just feels good.

Sunbathing pigeons have their own special pose. They often roll partly onto one side and stick a wing into the air. They spread their tails and fluff up their butt feathers. Staring into space, they contemplate the secrets of the universe that only pigeons know.

Molting

What you'll see: Feathers on the ground, and pigeons looking scruffier than usual.

Why it happens: Feathers accumulate dirt and damage. Then it's time to shed old feathers and grow new ones.

If you wear your favorite T-shirt every day, it'll pick up stains or holes. Soon, friends will start to hint—ever more strongly—that you should give that tee its well-deserved retirement to the back of the closet. Like your clothes, bird feathers need regular replacement. They accumulate stains, nibbles from parasites, or other structural damage. This doesn't just mar their otherwise scrupulous appearance; it makes them less useful for flying or keeping a bird warm.

Pigeons grow a whole new set of feathers about once a year. The old feathers don't fall out all at once, because a featherless pigeon would be flightless and cold (and horrifying). Instead, the feathers drop in a complex sequence called molting. For example, the wingtip feathers molt out one by one, from the innermost feathers to those at the tip. If a pigeon gets into trouble and loses some feathers—say, in a near miss with a hungry predator—it won't have to wait until the molt to replace them. So long as the entire feather has been pulled out, it'll start regrowing right away.

Molting is an intense process that costs a lot of energy. Some bird species molt at specific times of the year, avoiding energy-intensive periods like migration. Since pigeons are sedentary, they can molt at any time of the year, but they tend to do it in the summer and fall. They also slow their molt if they start reproducing, since it's hard to take care of babies *and* make sure you're wearing a clean T-shirt.

SOCIAL & ROMANTIC LIFE

Craving some drama and romance? Look no further than your local pigeons. Even during the coldest parts of the year, they flock, flirt, dance, and kiss each other (with their beaks *and* buttholes).

Flocking

What you'll see: Pigeons gathering, resting, and flying in groups.

Why it happens: While pigeons don't necessarily always hang out in flocks, flocking can help them stay safe and find food.

Flock this way!

If you're a prey animal that spends time in open areas, you may want to hang out with other vigilant prey animals who are scanning the landscape. When a falcon bursts into view and a flock of pigeons takes to the air, the predator has a harder time picking pigeons out of a tight, whirling flock than catching stragglers. Flocks are useful for another key reason: A pigeon that sticks around a flock is able to follow other birds to choice feeding sites.

Don't think of a pigeon flock as a tight-knit family of mutually supportive individuals, though. The social world of a flock is subtle and complex. Pigeons don't always flock, and when they do, the size of a flock may vary from a half-dozen birds to fifty or more. You may see a group of pigeons facing the same way when perched on a building, as if they're linked by a psychic bond, but they're just all facing into the wind so that their feathers don't get mussed. Flocking is about opportunity. Sometimes a bird will roost with one group but search for food with a different crowd, and it may nest in a colony of up to a thousand birds that occupy a shared space in a building. The whole thing is a real clusterflock.

Researchers have found that when flocks of homing pigeons travel back to their loft, some birds are more in charge of the navigation than others. This hierarchy can change over time and from flight to flight. According to a study by scientist Isobel Watts and colleagues, pigeons will even "demote" a top navigator who starts to mess up and become less reliable.

Males and Females

What you'll see: It's hard to tell male pigeons from females, especially if you're watching them from afar.

Why it happens: Pigeons don't have dangly genitals or obvious color differences between the sexes. But there are a few subtler signs you can look for.

Some animals make it easy. An 8,000-pound (3,700 kg) male southern elephant seal can weigh over four times more than a female. A female eclectus parrot is red and blue with a black bill, and a male is green with an orange bill; they look so different that scientists used to think they were two separate species. These obvious differences are called sexual dimorphism. But other creatures, like pigeons, are far less sexually dimorphic. Male and female pigeons come in pretty much the same colors. Males are larger, on average, and they have slightly bigger ceres (the fleshy lump over the beak). There are other small physical differences, too, but unless you're right up close to your pigeons, you may not spot them.

The best way to discern a pigeon's sex is to watch what it's doing. For the most part, males do a bit more of the cooing and all of the dancing and strutting (though there are exceptions). Male pigeons chase their mates away from other males. Also, pigeon pairs divide up their egg incubation duties in a special way. If you're watching a nest, you'll see the female sitting on eggs from the midafternoon and through the night until the morning. The male usually takes over for the rest of the time.

Monogamy

What you'll see: Pigeon pairs sticking together for better or for worse. (Mostly.)

Why it happens: Pigeons are lovebirds.

Let's face it: Mammals are bad at monogamy. Only a few—like the prairie vole, a scruffy brown rodent from central North America—form lasting pair bonds. Birds, on the other hand, are the romantics of the animal kingdom. Most make pair bonds that last through at least one breeding season.

Certain bird species stick together for life. These include Laysan albatrosses, bald eagles, mute swans, and even black vultures (picture them slurping on the same stringy bit of road-kill until their beaks meet in the middle). This sounds sweet, but monogamy can be pretty complicated. Plenty of birds are *socially* monogamous—they hang out and raise chicks together—but not *sexually* monogamous. For example, Laysan albatrosses frequently form female/female pairs. They'll sneak out to mate with other "monogamous" males and then return to their female partners to raise the resulting chicks.

Compared to many birds, pigeons are remarkably faithful. Sure, some of them switch mates after a season. And cheating does happen, but it's relatively rare. For the most part, pairs stick together both socially and sexually. You'll often see a male and female foraging side by side or snuggling up on a building ledge for a groom and a cuddle. Their bond lasts until death—which, unfortunately, can come quickly for a feral pigeon. Most don't live past three years of age. (A pampered pet pigeon, on the other hand, may survive for a decade or two.)

When one member of a feral pigeon pair dies, the other won't resign itself to a life of mourning. It'll dust off its dance moves and find a new partner.

Courtship, Part 1: Singing and Dancing

What you'll see: A pigeon bowing, strutting, cooing, and showing off.

Why it happens: If you want to woo a lady pigeon, you need to perform the right song and dance.

Are you ready to learn how to impress a female pigeon? Here are the steps. First, tell the world that you're ready for love: belt out a loud advertising coo. When a female arrives, inflate your crop so that your glossy neck plumes pop. Stand up as tall as you can, then bow deeply while making a display coo (scientists call this behavior the "bow coo"). Repeat these steps while strutting in a circle and dragging your flared tail along the ground.

You'll be judged. If the female finds your performance to be lacking, she'll fly away. If she's intrigued, she'll stick around for more courtship (and, eventually, sex). Nice job, Coo-sanova.

Courtship, Part 2: Mutual Preening

What you'll see: A pigeon gently nibbling its mate.

Why it happens: This behavior is called allopreening ("allo" comes from the Greek word *állos*, meaning "other"). It builds and reinforces bonds and keeps birds tidy.

Many birds preen each other, from penguins to parrots. They probably do it for the same reasons as us humans: Running your hand through your partner's hair is a gesture of comfort and bonding. Similarly, birds seem to allopreen to reduce stress. Pairs that allopreen are more cooperative in caring for their chicks.

There are more practical reasons to preen one's mate past the courtship phase. Birds often preen each other's head and neck regions in particular, helping to keep those hard-to-reach feathers in order. Plus, allopreening pigeons are effective at ridding each other of parasites. While you're stroking your lover's hair, you might as well check for ticks.

Courtship, Part 3: Kissing

What you'll see: Pigeons smooching.

Why it happens: They're not really smooching. They're pretending to puke into each other's mouths. Aww!

As a pigeon pair's courtship progresses, a female pigeon begins to act like a baby bird that needs to be fed. Fluttering her wings, she pecks the side of her mate's beak. The male opens his mouth wide, the female crams her bill in there, and the birds bob their heads as if they're retching. Why? Nobody's quite sure.

That beak-to-beak contact is also known as billing. Since olden times, people have used the expression "billing and cooing" to mean kissing and cuddling. Shakespeare's poem *Venus and Adonis* describes Venus's hand entrapping Adonis's hand as "two silver doves that sit a-billing."

After this beak-to-beak kissing, it's time for the main act. Yes, you guessed it: butthole kissing.

Courtship, Part 4: Doing the Deed

What you'll see: A pigeon climbing onto another pigeon's back and doing a lot of frantic flapping for a few seconds.

Why it happens: After all that chasing, strutting, and kissing, the actual act of copulation is simple and fast.

First, the female hunches down and raises her wings. The male hops on her back and starts flapping in a desperate attempt to stay on top of her. The female twists her tail aside to expose her cloaca, and the male twists his tail aside, too. He rubs the opening of his cloaca on hers in what's called the "cloacal kiss," ejaculates, then hops off. The whole thing lasts a few seconds.

You might scoff at their hastiness, but it's a good thing they do it quickly. Sometimes a jealous male pigeon sneaks up to a pair while they're having sex and tries to knock the copulating male off the female. Rude.

Showing off after Sex

What you'll see: A male pigeon swooping around and clapping its wings as if applauding itself for a deed well done.

Why it happens: Nobody's sure. Many animals display after sex.

After a pair of pigeons mates, the male often shows off. Standing up as tall as he can, he springs into the air and makes a short flight to a nearby perch. While flying, he flares his tail and alternates between clapping his wings in short bursts of three to five beats and gliding with his wings held up in a victorious *V.* He may repeat this display again and again, no matter how hard his partner rolls her eyes.

Scientists aren't sure why male pigeons do this postcopulatory maneuver. It may help strengthen the couple's bond or advertise to other birds that the pair is off the dating market. Ducks and shorebirds do postcopulatory displays, too. So do some bees and flies. (And certain humans.)

Driving

What you'll see: One pigeon chasing another.

Why it happens: Male pigeons herd, or "drive," their mates away from other males.

After a male and female mate but before the female has laid eggs, the pair tends to stick close together. During this blissful honeymoon, they may encounter lonely males who are looking for love. The male of the pair takes drastic steps to "defend" his partner: He chases her away from these would-be suitors.

Puffing up his crop to look huge, the male runs along behind the female, often pressing so close that he's stomping on her tail. Sometimes he even pecks vigorously at her head. Ouch. If she flies away, he follows, flying closely just behind and above her. He only stops harrying her once she's flown some distance away from the other birds or landed back at the nest.

Keeping the Romance Alive

What you'll see: An established pigeon pair running through their courtship behavior again and again.

Why it happens: Relationships thrive when a pair keeps the magic alive.

Everyone in a successful long-term partnership knows that relationships need care and maintenance. That's true even if you're *not* trying to raise two children on a narrow ledge above a busy street.

Pigeons tend to stick together for life, and during a breeding cycle, each partner must do his or her fair share of the chick-rearing duties or the young won't survive. Plus, when pigeons aren't actively breeding—say, if they take a break during the winter—they still need to work together to defend their chosen nest site from potential interlopers. They don't ever migrate, so they can't take a tropical vacation away from it all.

To keep their bond solid, members of established pairs regularly repeat their courtship rituals. But they don't always do it with the same enthusiasm. Sometimes they omit certain steps (like the bowing-strutting dance). You should never let the fires of passion burn out, but it's okay to let them simmer down a little.

Breeding Year-Round

What you'll see: Pigeons courting and making babies all through the year, even in the dead of winter.

Why it happens: Like humans, pigeons can have babies year-round. That's one reason why there are so many pigeons.

Plenty of birds, such as robins and warblers, only nest during certain seasons. They need nectar and insects to feed themselves and their young, and this fare is only available in the warmer months. Pigeons are different. Even in freezing weather, these crafty birds find trash to eat, and they can turn just about anything into nutritious milk for their babies. Plus, they don't nest in chilly, exposed tree branches. They prefer sheltered cavities, and often those warmed by human heating systems. We humans help them out by creating urban heat islands—cities that are relatively warmer than the surrounding wilds—and by dropping food waste year round.

Still, most pigeons won't breed in colder places during the dead of winter. Cold-weather breeding attempts are prone to failure, and they take up a lot of energy that a pigeon could use just to keep warm. But enough pigeons successfully rear winter babies that the behavior gets passed down through the generations.

On average, pigeons have about 6.5 broods of chicks per year (though they probably make more babies in warmer latitudes than in colder ones). Because they usually produce two chicks per brood, that's a lucky thirteen babies each year.

NESTS AND BABIES

Even in places where you'll see a lot of pigeons, you probably won't observe any fluffy chicks. Where are all the pigeon babies? The truth is, pigeons are pretty private about their nests and young. Here are the secrets of pigeon nests.

Picking a Nest Site

What you'll see: A pigeon doing an advertising coo while standing near a building, bridge, or other structure that has nest site potential.

Why it happens: The male pigeon is responsible for selecting the nest site, and he's looking for a sheltered area that will keep his babies safe.

You'll never see a pigeon nest cupped gently in the branches of a tree. Pigeons nest in human-built structures, a throwback to their pre-domestication days when they lived on cliffs. They especially prefer dark, cave-like places that are high up from the ground and sheltered from the wind. The floor of the nesting area has to be flat so it'll support the haphazard pile of sticks that they call a nest.

Some good nesting spots include ledges, ventilation shafts, rain gutters, rafters, abandoned buildings, barns, and grain elevators. On rare occasions, you'll see pigeons nesting in holes in trees, but they prefer to raise their babies in our buildings. It turns out we're quite good at making solid, rain-sheltered structures with flat floors—and our pigeony neighbors know it.

Defending the Nest Site

What you'll see: A pigeon pair attacking any other pigeons that stray into the area around their nest.

Why it happens: Once they've chosen a good nest site, a strongly bonded pair of pigeons will defend their territory from any and all interlopers.

When pigeons set up their nest, they define a territory around it. The exact size of the territory varies depending on the nest location and the number of other pigeons nesting nearby. Usually the defended area is pretty small—no bigger than 11 square feet or so (about a square meter). But the pair protects their tiny dominion with everything they've got. They swoop at intruders and kick them off their perches. They strike out with their wings. They do aggressive little bowing and flapping displays. They even peck trespassers on the head.

When a pair's bond is strong, both the male and the female join forces to defend the territory. But the male is the most active defender. He's especially aggressive in the days leading up to egg laying. Afterward, he chills out a bit, perhaps relaxing into the domestic bliss of fatherhood.

Building a Nest

What you'll see: Pigeons making haphazard, flimsy nests.

Why it happens: Some birds create elegant, complex nests. Pigeons do not.

Consider the female common tailorbird. To build her nest, this Southeast Asian bird carefully selects two living, green leaves. Without breaking the leaves from their twigs, she cuts minute holes in them and then delicately sews them together with spider silk and plant fibers. Down in the shady spot created by the

stitched foliage, the tailorbird builds a conical nest lined with soft plant fibers. And then there's the pigeon.

When a pigeon pair picks a nesting spot, the female sits there and urges the male to bring her sticks, straw, feathers, and other material that she arranges around herself in a loose disk. The resulting construction is best described by words such as "flimsy," "haphazard," and "bad." Some pairs don't even build a nest; they just lay eggs on their chosen ledge and sit on them. When the babies defecate, the parents don't remove the poop, so it builds up and solidifies the nest into a poopy pile. Once the young have fledged and the parents are ready to nest again, they often just reuse the old nest. They don't clear away the feces—or even broken eggs or dead chicks. Why bother? They just sit on top of it all, proud rulers of their poopy domain.

Laying Eggs

What you'll see: A mama pigeon straining to drop an egg from her cloaca.

Why it happens: All birds lay eggs that feed and house their young as they develop.

Before it gets laid, a pigeon egg goes on quite a journey. The trip begins in the ovary, where the egg develops its yolk (a food source for the growing chick). Then that egg moves down through a tube called the oviduct, where it develops its egg whites and meets up with the sperm to get fertilized. Next, it enters the shell gland and gains its hard coating. Finally, it pops out of the opening in that all-purpose poop/reproductive chamber, the cloaca. The process of pushing out the egg is incredibly fast. Blink and you'll miss it. If you're a human parent, this relatively easy process might make you jealous. (Get ready to become even more jealous: A female pigeon is ready to lay her eggs just eight to twelve days after mating.)

Pigeons usually produce two eggs per breeding cycle, spacing them about forty hours apart. The oval-shaped eggs are creamy white and about 1.5 inches (3.8 cm) long, close to the size of Ping-Pong balls. If you're watching a pigeon nest, you'll rarely catch a glimpse of them. The parents keep their precious treasure covered almost all the time.

Sitting on Eggs

What you'll see: Mom and dad pigeons taking turns sitting on the nest.

Why it happens: Eggs need warmth and protection so their embryos can properly develop.

Before the eggs arrive, pigeon parents sometimes practice their incubation skills. They'll sit on the nest for an hour or two, then leave. But once the eggs are laid, crap gets real. A pigeon embryo takes about twenty days to turn into a chick and hatch out of its egg, and the parents need to keep it warm and protect it from hungry predators that whole time. This endeavor is deadly serious, and pigeon parents do not mess around.

Both parents share the responsibility of incubation, but they divvy it up by time of day. The female sits on the eggs from late afternoon through the night and into the midmorning. Then she goes to find food or bathe or otherwise take a break, and the male pigeon incubates the eggs from midmorning to late afternoon (he doesn't get to sleep on the nest). The parents keep their eggs covered for more than 99 percent of the day. When they swap incubating duties, they leave the eggs uncovered for a maximum of two minutes, but usually less.

Pigeons take incubation seriously—maybe too seriously. Sometimes house sparrows pull feathers from the butts of nesting pigeons to line their nests. The pigeons weather this injustice stoically and just keep on incubating their eggs.

Hatching

What you'll see: A parent pigeon shifting around anxiously as if something exciting is about to happen.

Why it happens: Hatching isn't just about breaking an egg. It's a big event in a bird's life—a complex process that takes a long time and a lot of energy.

Even if you're keeping a close eye on a pigeon nest, you may not see the babies hatch. That's because the parents keep them warm and hidden throughout the whole process. But you'll notice that the sitting parent seems to get anxious, frequently standing and then sitting down. That anxiety is justified. Hatching is intense and there's so much that can go wrong.

A chick inside an egg has to go through a lot of physical preparation before it can even start chipping away at the shell. For most of its time in the egg, it breathes oxygen that filters through the shell. But the egg also contains a pocket of air, and as the baby pigeon gets ready to hatch, it breaks into this pocket to breathe. It also cuts off its contact with the blood vessels lining the shell and pulls the remaining blood into its body. Finally, the chick absorbs the last of the yolk, and now it's ready to be born.

For this part, the baby pigeon has a custom-made tool to help it along: a hard tip at the end of its beak called an egg tooth. The chick taps the tooth against the shell to make a crack and then slowly moves around to expand it. A lot of time—up to a day—can elapse between that first crack and the baby's emergence. Plenty of chicks don't survive this harrowing experience.

Feeding Milk to Their Young

What you'll see: Baby pigeons shoving their heads down their parents' throats.

Why it happens: Mammals aren't the only animals that make milk for their babies. Both mom and dad pigeons produce milk, and it gives their chicks a nutritious boost.

Pour yourself a frosty glass of pigeon milk. Or maybe don't. Pigeon milk, or crop milk, is a secretion produced in the lining of a pigeon's throat. It doesn't have the same texture as cow milk; it's cheesier and more curd-like. Since pigeons don't have nipples, mom and dad pigeons have to puke this milk into their kids' throats. For the first three or so days of a baby pigeon's life, it consumes only crop milk. After that, it starts getting a little barfed-up seed, too.

horrrrrrrrrrk

Pigeon milk may be a little chunky, but it shares a few key similarities with human milk. A hormone called prolactin stimulates milk production in both pigeons and people. Plus, crop milk isn't just rich in protein and fat. Like human milk, it also has antioxidants and immune boosters.

Scientists have figured out which genes are responsible for making crop milk, which means that they could theoretically produce it on a large scale someday. When civilization collapses, maybe the last survivors will subsist on glasses of chunky pigeon milk.

Babies Growing

What you'll see: The pigeon parents caring for a pair of awkward-looking, partly naked, partly yellow-feathered chicks.

Why it happens: When pigeon babies hatch, they're blind and helpless and look nothing like adult pigeons.

Eight Days

Eighteen Days

The more culinary-conscious among us may know the word "squab" in reference to pigeon meat. Squab is young pigeon. Baby pigeons are called squabs until they're thirty days old. All kids are awkward, but squabs are especially goofy looking. They have long, knobbly beaks and striking coats of sparse white-yellow fluff. For the first five days, their eyes haven't yet opened and their wings are just fleshy stubs that they use to push themselves around the nest. They can't keep themselves warm enough to survive, so they press close to their sibling and parents to absorb their body heat.

Over time, though, a squab gets bigger and stronger. Soon it can stretch out its neck and whistle stridently to demand another barfed-up meal from mom and dad. It begins to grow its first real feathers, and after a couple of weeks, it's able to walk. When it hits the age of three or four weeks, it starts practicing its wing flaps. Then, only a month or so after it emerges from its egg, it leaves the nest, a fresh-faced young pigeon in a big new world.

Leaving the Nest and Growing Up

What you'll see: A young, fully feathered pigeon leaving the nest but still begging for food from its parents.

Why it happens: All too soon, it's time for a young pigeon to make its own way in the world—but, like most young adults, it still needs a little help from mom and dad.

The exact date of a pigeon's departure from its nest varies. When the weather is warm, a bird may fledge at twenty-eight days; in the middle of winter, it may hunker down in the warmth of its nest for forty-five days.

When a young pigeon flaps its way out of its nest, it's no longer a squab. Now it's called a fledgling. It spends a couple of weeks hanging around its parents, begging for food and trying to make sense of its baffling new surroundings. Over time, it copies the feeding and drinking behavior of adults. By seven weeks it's able to feed itself. Its voice starts to "break" and soon

it can make adult coos. Young birds have the same general size and shape of adults, but there are a few key differences you can look for (learn about them on page 181).

Once a young bird is ready to make its own nest, will it stick close to home or fly the coop to join another breeding colony? Scientists aren't sure. Pigeon youths definitely wander around a lot more than adults. Some youngsters settle down close to their hatching site, and others travel farther, but nobody knows exactly how far they go on average. Once they get there, though, they waste no time in making new pigeons. The age of sexual maturity is pretty variable, but birds can start to pair up when they're only six to eight months old. All too soon, the newly adult pigeons are dancing, strutting, and building their terrible nests, completing the circle of life and adding new pages to the bizarre book of feral pigeon history.

PIGEON TROUBLESHOOTING

How to Stay Healthy and Help Pigeons

Pigeons are our neighbors, but sometimes neighbors rub us the wrong way. Maybe a pigeon pair is nesting on your balcony and pooping everywhere while refusing to chip in a single dollar for the rent. Or perhaps you've found an injured pigeon and you want to know how to help it survive. Maybe you've already named your injured pigeon—she's called Lady Fluffington of the Coo Manor Fluffingtons—and you need to get the lady to a good doctor before she succumbs to the vapors. Help is on the way. Here's a quick guide to pigeon problems and solutions.

WILL PIGEONS MAKE ME SICK?

Are pigeons disease-ridden pests? Since so many of us spend our lives in close proximity to these birds, it's reasonable to worry that they'll make us ill. Fear not. Those concerns are, for the most part, unfounded.

For a study published in the *Journal of Infection*, Swiss researchers Daniel Haag-Wackernagel and Holger Moch sifted through the medical literature to identify cases where pigeons had spread infections to people, and they found that the risk is low. Though pigeons have been shown to carry sixty dangerous microorganisms that can harm humans, the scientists found records of only seven of them being transmitted to people. The most commonly spread pathogens were the bacterium *Chlamydia psittaci* and the fungus *Cryptococcus neoformans*. In most cases, these infections occur when humans inhale aerosolized bird excretions, though some cases of psittacosis (infection by *C. psittaci*) can be traced back to handling sick or dead birds or feeding pigeons. In rarer cases, people can get salmonellosis or toxoplasmosis from pigeons.

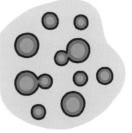

Cryptococcus neoformans

Other studies show that pigeon parasites can cause trouble; their ticks may bite people and cause a rare but dangerous allergic reaction. But overall, as Haag-Wackernagel and Moch found, there's minimal risk of infection. Other researchers have discovered that pigeons aren't effective at spreading bird flus like H5N1. If you're walking around and observing pigeons, or sharing space with them in a park, the danger is vanishingly small. (If your job or hobby exposes you to a lot of pigeons or pigeon poop, exercise caution and take action to protect yourself from infections.)

Why are pigeons relatively harmless? One major reason is evolutionary. Many parasites and pathogens have evolved to afflict specific targets, and it's hard for some of them to jump between groups of distantly related critters, like birds and mammals. For instance, pigeons can't give you rabies—but mammals like dogs, bats, and raccoons can.

One important note: If your immune system is weakened due to an illness or a medical treatment like chemotherapy, be especially careful around pigeons. Your immunocompromised state puts you at much greater risk of infection.

WHY DO SO MANY PIGEONS HAVE MESSED-UP FEET?

You'll often see pigeons missing one or more toes. Some of them hobble around on stumps. This toe loss can come from disease or injury, but there's another, more sinister explanation. Our cities and towns are full of stray bits of thread and hair. When this material tangles around a pigeon's toes, the bird isn't able to remove it. The string tightens until the toe loses its blood supply and falls off. Rates of so-called "stringfoot" are higher in places with more people, more pollution, and less green space. Pigeons may be especially susceptible to this type of injury because they walk instead of hop, so their feet spend more time on the ground.

WHY DON'T I SEE LOTS OF DEAD PIGEONS?

If you read about pigeons on the internet—who doesn't do this all the time, especially on a lonely Saturday night?—then you'll soon encounter a frequently asked question: "Where are all the dead pigeons?" Though many places like busy public squares are packed with pigeons, we rarely see dead birds. Does a secret force of pigeon undertakers whisk them away in the night?

Sort of. There are tons of critters that eat carrion (dead animals), even deep in a city, and they're always scanning for fresh meat. Some of them operate during the day, such as gulls, crows, and magpies. Others are most active when it's dark, including foxes, raccoons, and feral cats. This army of scavengers makes short work of a deceased bird as soon as it hits the pavement.

There's another factor at work. Sick pigeons tend to hide in sheltered places away from predators. If they die, they do so out of sight.

HOW DO I STOP PIGEONS FROM NESTING ON MY BALCONY OR WINDOWSILL?

Sometimes pigeons lay eggs in undesirable places. Their nesting materials can block rain gutters. Even worse, their poop can foul up buildings, a noxious phenomenon that may cause more than a billion dollars in damages every year in the United States alone. Plus, sometimes their amorous cooing is *very* enthusiastic. To prevent pigeons from nesting in a particular spot, try to keep your property neat and tidy. Pigeons like to nest in protected locations, so consider removing any potential shelter like furniture or other objects when they're not in use. Scare away pigeons by hanging strips of shiny paper, putting up pinwheels, or, if the birds are on a balcony, just walking around—your presence will spook them. Since pigeons nest on flat surfaces, you can try adjusting any potential nesting surface so that it has a slant. Nobody wants to store eggs on a ramp.

Here are some things you *shouldn't* do. Don't buy a bunch of bird netting and wrap it around your balcony. All sorts of birds and other animals can get tangled in the netting and die, which is terrible for both the critters and you. Also, think twice before putting up plastic owl decoys. Feral pigeons get used to them after a while.

If the pigeons already have chicks, wait until they leave the nest before trying to shoo the birds away. Don't move the babies or otherwise separate them from the parents—the babies will die. Luckily, you won't have to wait long. Depending on the season (see page 182), the young are ready to go after just four weeks or so.

PIGEON POOP VS. ASTRONOMY

In 1964, two astronomers heard a strange staticky sound from a microwave antenna, a big horn-shaped device they were using to listen to radio signals from space. They investigated and found pigeons nesting inside. Oh no. The astronomers tried to relocate the pigeons, but the birds kept returning. Eventually, and with great reluctance, the astronomers shot them. But the noise was still there. It wasn't a glitch—it was cosmic microwave background radiation, a remnant from the Big Bang. The astronomers, Arno Penzias and Robert Wilson, earned a Nobel Prize for their discovery.

HELP—THERE'S A PIGEON TRAPPED IN MY BUILDING!

Sometimes a pigeon flies into a building and can't find its way out. If this happens, open up a single exit and close all the other potential exits. Don't try to chase the bird; it'll panic. Instead, turn off the lights to calm the animal and make the way out more visible. Urge everyone to leave the area to let the bird find its way back out into the wild.

HELP—I FOUND A PET PIGEON!

You may come across a pigeon that doesn't look like it belongs with the rest of the flock. If it acts tame and has fancy plumage, it could be an escaped pet. Such wayward domestics are very likely to end up as cat or hawk food. Their unusual looks draw the eyes of predators; plus, they don't know how to survive in the wild, and they're often less adept at flying than their feral cousins. Here's how to tell if you've found a pet bird instead of a feral:

- **Your pigeon has a band:**
  To keep track of their birds, some pigeon keepers put bands—thick metal or plastic bracelets—around their birds' legs. If you find a bird with a band, it belongs to somebody.

She's with the band.

It could be a racing pigeon that ran into trouble on its way home, or it could be a beloved house pet that accidentally found its way outside. Consider catching it and taking it to a wildlife rehabilitator, wildlife center, animal shelter, or other safe place for help. In the United States, you can look up the numbers and letters on a pigeon band and report a lost bird on the website of the American Racing Pigeon Union at pigeon.org/lostbirdinfo.htm

• **Your pigeon is fancy:** You may find an escaped bird that isn't banded but has fancy plumage. It may act overly friendly, hanging out near people as if begging for food or help. If you suspect you've come across someone's wayward fancy pigeon, you may want to help it find a home.

HELP—I FOUND AN INJURED PIGEON!

If you find a hurt bird, consider rescuing it. How can you tell if it's hurt? The signs may be obvious, like regurgitating, bleeding, shaking, oil-soaked feathers, or body parts twisted in the wrong direction. They may be more subtle: An adult bird that's hunched on the ground and doesn't react when you approach is ill or injured. And then there's the issue of cat scratches. If a cat so much as bats at a pigeon, that bird needs medical attention. Even small scratches transmit the bacterium *Pasteurella multocida*, which causes deadly blood poisoning.

Just don't put a bird's safety ahead of your own—for instance, never run into a busy road to perform a daring rescue!

HELP—I FOUND A LOST BABY PIGEON!

So cute! Should you bundle it up in a blanket, carry it home to live with you forever, and name it in memory of Grandpa George, even though Grandpa George is still alive and that'll make things super awkward at the family reunion?

Not so fast. Caring for a pigeon chick is hard. First off, the chick needs to drink its parents' milk. Rescuers who nurse baby pigeons feed them a complex fluid that matches this milk as closely as possible. You also have to learn the proper technique for feeding a young pigeon; if you do it incorrectly, you could send food or fluid into the bird's lungs, making it sick. You're far better off getting your bird to a trained professional who can give it the best start to life. George will thank you. (Both Georges, really.)

First, though, you should look for the bird's nest. If you can see it, put the baby back inside. Don't worry—its parents won't reject it because it smells like a human! If you can't find the nest, then it's time to swoop to the rescue.

While you work on finding someone who can take in the bird, build it a temporary home. Grab a shoebox (or similarly sized box), cut air holes into it, insert some soft fabric, and tuck the baby pigeon inside. Put the box in a warm, dark place. If you can, get a heating pad, turn it on low, and slide it under half of the box (the baby needs to be able to waddle away from the heat if it gets too warm). As soon as you're able, get the bird to someone who can help.

Congratulations! All of your late-night shoe purchases are now justified.

HOW DO I CATCH OR PICK UP A PIGEON THAT NEEDS HELP?

The San Francisco–based nonprofit group Palomacy (a portmanteau of "pigeon diplomacy") saves pigeons and provides adoption services. They've got tons of useful tips for catching pigeons in need. But first, they offer assurance to would-be pigeon heroes: A distressed pigeon won't hurt you. Also, it's unlikely to make you sick (but see page 186 for more info about pigeon pathogens). You may worry that catching a pigeon will give the bird a heart attack, but pigeons are made of tougher stuff. Think of those pigeon war heroes who flew through artillery fire. Here's how to catch a pigeon:

- **If your pigeon is a baby, seriously injured, or extremely chill around people:** Just scoop it up with both hands. Wrap your hands gently around its body with its wings folded against its sides.

- **If your pigeon is nervous but can't fly away:** Drop a towel, sheet, or piece of clothing over the bird. This will confuse it, and then you can scoop it up.

- **If your pigeon is standoffish and able to fly away:** It's time to set a trap. Get a crate or cage (a dog cage works well) and tie a string to the door so that you can pull it closed from afar. Make a trail of bait leading up to the cage and place more bait deep inside. Since pigeons love grains and legumes, you can bait your trap with birdseed, rice, quinoa, lentils, or other similar foods. When the bird wanders into the trap, pull the door shut. If the bird panics, don't worry—just cover the cage with a blanket to calm it down.

- **If none of these techniques are successful:** The Palomacy website (pigeonrescue.org) offers a host of other ideas.

I CAUGHT A TROUBLED PIGEON. WHAT DO I DO WITH IT?

Good work, pigeon wrangler! Now you need to transport your bird to someone who can help it. Do a little research and figure out your options. There may be a wildlife care center nearby, or even one devoted specically to wild birds. If you can't find one, search for wildlife rehabilitators (individual people who are trained to care for injured or orphaned wildlife). If you're stuck,

THE GLITZY TALE OF THE RHINESTONE PIGEON

In 2018, a concerned citizen in Glendale, Arizona, came across a pigeon wearing a rhinestone-studded vest. Baffled, she caught it and brought it to a bird rescue center. The center's owner posted a picture of the bird online, and the image of the bejeweled bird went viral. Soon, the Rhinestone Pigeon—actually named Olive, and actually wearing a rhinestone-studded diaper—was reunited with her overjoyed owners.

look for wildlife information hotlines and call one. If you think you've found someone's pet bird, try your local animal shelter. But be sure to ask the rehabilitator or care center whether they care for pigeons. Some groups accept only native birds and refuse to take in feral pigeons.

SHOULD I FEED THE PIGEONS IN THE PARK?

This is a hard question, and it's a topic that stirs up a lot of emotions for many people. In outdoor plazas around the world, tourists feed pigeons and take selfies with birds on their arms. Vendors sell pigeon food, sometimes illegally. Some cities have banned pigeon feeding, and rogue pigeon feeders respond by distributing birdseed under cover of darkness. There's a lot of frustration, worry, and anger on all sides. It's all very complex and heartbreaking.

The desire to feed pigeons is totally reasonable—it's a way to connect with nature and with other bird-loving people. But if you're worried that your local pigeons will starve without your help, consider this: When you feed pigeons, you encourage them to make more pigeons. The size of their population depends on the amount of available food. Overpopulation can cause crowding and encourage disease transmission. Plus, more birds mean more poop. Some people who feed pigeons also clean up their droppings, but most don't or can't.

We have a moral responsibility to treat animals humanely. Some of us (including this author) had ancestors who domesticated, bred, transported, and released pigeons, so we must care for these feral creatures we've created. As the fox in Antoine de Saint-Exupéry's *The Little Prince* says, "You become responsible, forever, for what you have tamed." But feeding animals an appropriate diet is a big responsibility and takes a lot of knowledge and understanding. There are plenty of other ways to tend to the animals around you and treat them kindly. For instance, you can rescue injured birds, clean up potential hazards (like bird netting, sticky traps, string, or patches of oil that can trap birds and coat feathers), and support your heroic local wildlife rehabilitators.

CAN I ADOPT A PET PIGEON?

If you're ready to take your love of pigeons to the next level, there are plenty of pet pigeons in animal shelters. Bring one home today! You can keep your adopted friend in an outdoor aviary or inside your house. Make sure it has a large cage, access to a bathing dish, a basket to cozy up in, and shelves to perch on. Give it plenty of socialization, either with people or with other pet pigeons. A pigeon is a calm, gentle pet that tends to keep to itself—like a cat, but less likely to shred your sofa. Some birds like to be petted on the head and neck (allopreened, really).

What about poop? Well, as we learned from the tale of the rhinestone pigeon (see page 196), a number of pigeon-specific stores offer pigeon pants—basically fancy bird diapers, complete with a disposable lining and a tail hole. Even better: They come in a variety of fashionable prints. The company Avian Fashions, for example, sells diapers (they call them FlightSuits) in plaid, denim, holiday-appropriate hues like orange for Halloween, and much more. Do pigeons enjoy wearing diapers? They get used to it. Palomacy calls diapered pigeons "very good sports," and it's hard to disagree.

That's just a speedy intro to pigeon adoption. Before you bring one home, you'll need to learn more about the specifics (like behavioral training, cage size, veterinary care, appropriate feed, and more). Do your reading, reach out to experts, and search online for other pigeon keepers who can help you out. Soon your home will be full of gentle cooing, and you'll have a drawer of colorful pigeon diapers on hand for every holiday.

The splendor of pigeon pants.

OTHER BIRDS WORTH WATCHING

Are you ready to branch out? Pigeon watching is your gateway to the vast world of birdwatching, also known as birding. You can use your newfound skills to help you find majestic peregrine falcons, elegant native doves, and many other fascinating feathered neighbors.

TIP 1: USE PIGEONS TO FIND PIGEON PREDATORS

Where there be pigeons, there be predators. Raccoons, house cats, weasels, opossums, and many other creatures readily eat them. A pigeon's greatest threat, though, is death from above. The skies are full of pigeon hunters.

Birds of prey—properly called raptors—live almost everywhere, even in the depths of the city. In fact, some raptors gravitate to urban environments; they enjoy nesting on high rises and eating the abundant pigeons and sparrows. They're amazing to watch, but they can be hard to find. Many of them are shy and quiet, which makes sense because they rely on surprise to outwit their prey. Often your only glimpse of raptors will be of

---

EAT PREY: DOVE

Besides hawks and falcons, many types of birds snack on pigeons from time to time. They include:

- Crows and ravens (e.g., common ravens and carrion crows)
- Eagles (e.g., golden eagles)
- Gulls (e.g., glaucous-winged gulls)
- Kites (e.g., red kites—yes, a kite is a bird as well as a toy)
- Owls (e.g., great-horned owls and screech owls)

---

dark silhouettes soaring high overhead, trying to be inconspicuous as they scan the area.

But birdwatchers have a secret technique to locate raptors: They look for pigeons. Seriously. If you see a flock of pigeons burst into the air and wheel around at speed, odds are there's a bird of prey nearby. Keep watching and you may catch a shocking moment of drama as the raptor dives to catch dinner.

Some pigeon predators, like the world's fastest animal, the peregrine falcon, are found all over the world. Others, like the Cooper's hawk, North America's terrorizer of bird feeders, are a little more localized. Here are a few predators you may see. Consult a field guide to learn which raptors live in your area!

Falcons

Falcons are built for speed, and many have dark facial markings that give them a goth look. Falcons that snack on pigeons to varying degrees include gyrfalcons, aplomado falcons, prairie falcons, lanner falcons, Eurasian kestrels, and others.

What's the difference between a falcon and another superficially similar bird of prey, like a hawk or eagle? Amazingly, falcons aren't so closely related to those other birds of prey. They independently evolved their sharp talons and wickedly curved beaks. It's often difficult to tell a falcon from a hawk, but look for a falcon's slender, pointed wings instead of a hawk's rounder wings.

Example: Peregrine Falcon

Found on every continent except Antarctica, the peregrine falcon dives at speeds of more than 200 miles per hour (322 kph)—faster than a cheetah and on par with a Formula 1 race car.

What it looks like: A peregrine falcon is pale below and dark above, with a black mark stretching down from its eye. Young birds have browner plumage and paler feet.

How it hunts: Incredibly, this hunter is able to catch and kill prey entirely in the air. If a peregrine encounters a flying flock of pigeons, it hassles the birds at the edges, trying to split some of them off from the safety of the group. When it comes within striking distance, it grabs its prey with its massive talon-tipped feet and, while still flying, bites into its neck. Using a pair of points on its upper beak called tomial teeth, it severs the prey's spinal column. It does all of this without touching the ground. Ruthless.

Accipiters

Accipiters (that's "ack-SIP-it-ers") have more rounded wings. This trait, plus their long, rudder-like tails, give many species the agility they need to hunt birds in forested areas. Look for their characteristic flight pattern: a few flaps, then a glide. Several species eat pigeons, including the largest, the northern goshawk, which prefers to lurk in mature forests but inhabits urban parks in places like Berlin, Helsinki, and Tokyo.

Example: Cooper's Hawk

If you live in North America and some hawk keeps stealing the birds from your bird feeder, chances are it's a Cooper's hawk. This is a bird-eating specialist, and in urban centers, it's a major pigeon harasser.

What it looks like: The Cooper's hawk is slate gray above and rusty red below, with orange or red eyes, long legs, and a slender, stripy tail. Young birds are speckled brown with dark teardrop-shaped streaks on their chests.

How it hunts: A Coop can catch its prey on the ground or in the air. It doesn't bite its victim. Instead, it kills with its feet. Holding its prey at the end of its slender legs, it digs in its talons, squeezing and squeezing until its victim dies. Again—ruthless.

Buteos

Ah, to be a lazy hawk, slowly circling higher and higher, like a kite on the wind. If you see a raptor doing this, it may be a buteo ("BYOO-tee-oh"). Called hawks in the Americas and buzzards in Europe, Africa, and Asia, these birds tend to have sturdy bodies, broad and rounded wings, and shorter tails (though there's plenty of variation). Examples of buteos include the common buzzard and the rough-legged hawk. Most of them eat a lot of mammals, but they'll snack on birds if the opportunity arises—and in pigeon-filled urban areas, the opportunity definitely arises.

Example: Red-Tailed Hawk

North Americans are lucky that this huge, gorgeous hawk with a brick-red tail is a common species. In rural settings, it's often seen hunting from perches like fence posts and telephone poles. But across the continent, it has become habituated to city life. This has earned it many admirers; for instance, there are multiple books about a beloved New York City redtail named Pale Male who once nested near Central Park. On the other hand, people get alarmed when a red-tailed hawk plunks a dead pigeon onto the hood of their car and starts to chow down. There's no satisfying some folks.

What it looks like: Red-tailed hawks vary a lot by location; some have bright chests marked with a dark belly band, and others are almost all dark brown. Most, but not all, have rich red tails. Young birds always have brown-striped tails instead.

How it hunts: It swoops down on prey that's sitting on the ground and crushes it in its enormous talons, some of which can measure more than 1.33 inches (3.3 cm) in length. Whoof.

TIP 2: LOOK FOR OTHER KINDS OF PIGEONS

Once you start watching feral pigeons, you'll begin to notice other pigeon-type birds hanging out in places frequented by people. Many members of Columbidae have learned to inhabit our cities, towns, and farms, eating our spilled food and visiting our bird feeders, cooing us awake in the wee hours of the morning.

These birds are not always as numerous as the ferals, but they're equally intriguing, and many of them are downright spectacular. Plus, some of them are only found in specific parts of the world, so you can appreciate them as local specialties. Here are some other pigeons and doves to watch.

BIRDWATCHING IS A BIG DEAL

In the United States alone, birdwatching contributes an estimated $41 billion to the economy annually. More than 45 million Americans watch birds at home or on trips abroad. There are birdwatching apps, board games, festivals, songs, art contests, and spotting competitions. Birding is for everyone, and many diversity-boosting initiatives are making the hobby more welcoming to birdwatchers from marginalized communities. These include Black Birders Week and the National Audubon Society's Let's Go Birding Together, an LGBT-inclusive initiative.

Eurasian Collared-Dove

This big, blunt-tailed dove is native to much of Europe and Asia—but in the 1970s it was introduced to New Providence, Bahamas. It spread like the hot pants craze, but unlike hot pants, it

has endured. Now you can hear the Eurasian collared-dove's loud koo-KOO-kook throughout much of the Caribbean and North America.

Mourning Dove

Smaller than a feral pigeon, the mourning dove is arguably more elegant, with a pointed tail and a pale, peach-colored head and breast. This bird is named for its deep, mournful coo, which can sound a lot like an owl's hoot. It's notorious for laying its eggs in flimsy, rickety nests, making birdwatchers really nervous when the wind blows hard.

Eared Dove

This bird looks a lot like a mourning dove except that it has *enormous* ears. Just kidding. It has little black dots over its ears, plus a shorter tail than a mourning dove. You'll find it across much of South America. Like the mourning dove, it's a popular game bird and vigorously hunted.

Common Wood Pigeon

Found in parts of Europe, western Asia, and northern Africa, this exceedingly chunky bird looks like a feral pigeon that got hit with some kind of sci-fi expansion ray. It often hangs out in parks or on farms, where it waddles along the ground eating plants and small critters. The more northern and eastern populations migrate to warmer lands during the winter.

Crested Pigeon

At one time, you could only find this pointy-headed, glossy-winged pigeon in Australia's dry, sparsely treed grasslands. But then European settlers cleared forests, and the crested pigeon spread readily into settlements, agricultural areas, and any ranchland with watering holes. Now it's found throughout most of the country.

Speckled Pigeon

The word "speckled" doesn't do this bird justice. It has silver and maroon plumage with bright spots and a ring of red skin around its eyes. Once confined to wild, rocky habitats, this African species has been moving into cities, especially in South Africa. You can also find it eating seeds on farms. Amazingly, it likely interbred with our feral pigeon to produce the T-check and check wing patterns (see page 118 for more).

Zebra Dove

This heavily striped bird is native to
Southeast Asia—but because it's a
popular pet and readily goes feral,
nobody's quite sure about the
extent of its original native range.
You'll find feral zebra doves
pecking at your feet in Laos,
Hawaii, Tahiti, and plenty of
other places.

Oriental Turtle-Dove

The Oriental turtle-dove has
nothing whatsoever to do with
turtles. Its name comes from
the Latin word *turtur*, which may
be an imitation of its *turrrr, turrrr*
cooing sound. Its wings have a
pretty scalloped pattern, and it
boasts a fancy patch of zebra-
striped plumage on its neck.
It's widespread across much
of Asia.

African Collared-Dove

Besides the feral pigeon, one other member of
the pigeon family was domesticated a long,
long time ago: the African collared-
dove. You might see one as part of
a magician's act. ("Hey, where'd
those doves come from, and
how much dove poop is in that
magician's pockets?") Named
for the black ring that partly encircles
its neck, it's found in sub-Saharan Africa.

TIP 3: LOOK FOR OTHER BIRDS—AND OBSERVE THEIR PLUMAGE VARIATIONS

Not to freak you out, but wherever you live, you're surrounded
by birds. Some of these birds aren't native to your area, such
as the house sparrows you'll find in North America (they're
from Europe, Africa, or Asia) or the surly Canada geese that
haunt parks in Europe (they're native to land all across North
America, so you can't just blame Canada, eh). Others are native.
Certain birds may hang out near you year-round, while others visit only in certain parts of the year, or just pass through
during migration. Some of them are unique to your particular
part of the globe.

You can find tons of great books, apps, clubs, and online guides that'll help you learn about the birds you see and hear around you. But your pigeon-watching skills have already prepared you for your new hobby: You can now spot amazing variations in plumage colors and patterns.

Native wild birds don't vary in color as much as feral pigeons, whose hues and patterns come from centuries of careful selective breeding, enhancing, and shaping of random mutations. But males and females of many species often differ, and some come in a few different plumages. Plus, the occasional wild bird is born with a pigment abnormality that elevates it from ordinary to astonishing. Use your pigeon-spotting skills to observe some of the following special plumages.

Sex Differences

Males and females of certain bird species look wildly different.

Example: Female northern cardinals are olive with a few red spots. Males are almost completely red. Though the male birds have a reputation for singing sweetly, both cardinal sexes sing. This is true of a lot of bird species, but science has long ignored female birdsong.

*Female
Northern Cardinal*

*Male
Northern Cardinal*

Seasonal Differences

Some birds change their looks from season to season to suit their shifting needs. They may develop fancy plumage when it's time to find a mate, then molt all that finery once they've passed on their genes and moved beyond the need to impress. A male pin-tailed whydah, for example, grows a very long tail during the breeding season, nearly tripling its total length. Other birds change color to blend in with background vegetation; arctic birds called ptarmigans, for instance, are white during snowy winters and brown during snow-free summers.

Example: European starlings are speckled in the fall and winter. During the spring and summer, when they're trying to look nice for their mates, they're darker with an iridescent rainbow sheen.

*Non-breeding
Plumage*

Breeding Plumage

Age Differences

Young birds can look rather different from older birds, even when they grow large enough to match their parents in size. In some cases, the difference is subtle, like a slight greenish tinge or a bit of brownish plumage. In other cases, it's dramatic. Some juvenile gulls, for instance, are brown all over, while adults have crisp white and gray plumage. Once you identify youngsters, you may notice them acting more awkward than their older counterparts. It's sort of like a bird wearing a sticker that says "New Driver: Please Be Patient."

Example: Bald eagles don't earn their "bald" white heads until they turn four or five. Juveniles have brown heads, and people often mistake them for golden eagles.

Juvenile Bald Eagle

Adult Bald Eagle

Regional Differences

Sometimes birds of the same species look remarkably different depending on where you are in the world.

Example: Dark-eyed juncos, an intriguing little species of North American sparrow, come in a handful of color patterns that vary by geographical location. For instance, birds on the west coast of North America have black heads and brown sides, while birds in the east are dark gray.

Many shades of junco.

Morphs

Some birds come in a few very distinct color types, called morphs.

Example: European honey-buzzards are some of the most variable raptors in the world; they have at least ten different color patterns, from dark chocolate brown to streaky to white.

Dark Morph

Pale Morph

Feather Pigment Abnormalities

A white raven? A blond bald eagle? Believe it. Feather pigment abnormalities can cause striking color forms. These include:

- **Albino:** birds that have a mutation preventing them from producing melanin pigment, so their feathers are white and their eyes are pink; they have vision problems

- **Melanistic:** birds with abnormal deposits of melanin, so they look darker

- **Fully or partially leucistic:** birds that lack melanin-producing cells; they may be partially or fully white, and their eyes may be normal-colored or darker; their eyesight is normal

- **Brown:** birds with partially light-sensitive pigment that bleaches out in sunlight

*Regular
Black-billed
Magpie*

*Brown
Black-billed
Magpie*

Examples: Black-billed magpies are stunning black-and-white birds belonging to the crow family. Birdwatchers sometimes encounter individuals whose feathers are pale brown. In this case, a melanin pigment has been chemically altered so that it looks brown instead of black and bleaches when exposed to the sun.

Health and Dietary Differences

A bird's diet and health can influence the color and condition of its feathers, sometimes with striking results.

Normal House Finch

Yellow House Finch

Example: Male house finches usually have red plumage, but poor health or a diet of food low in carotenoid pigments can cause variations in the intensity of that redness—some individuals are even yellow instead of red! Similarly, cedar waxwings that eat the berries of a certain type of honeysuckle will grow tails with orange tips instead of yellow ones.

The end, anatomically speaking.

CONCLUSION

This is it. You've reached the end of this book—its cloaca, if you will.

We live in tough times. These times call for superheroes, and pigeons can't save the world. Gone are the days when a well-timed carrier pigeon message could pull people back from the brink of destruction. But pigeons do have some significant superpowers: They can lighten the load while you work to make the world a better place. They connect you with the hidden life around you and teach you about biology, from its most beautiful parts (that iridescent neck sheen!) to the depths of its grossness (that chunky pigeon milk!). They open the door to all sorts of riveting history and elucidate the ways we interact with animals and with each other, for good and for bad.

When we begin to care about creatures that most people think are lowly, we become better people. We weave ourselves more tightly into the tapestry of the world around us, and we arm ourselves for the fight to save the world.

So, thank you for joining the flock on this journey. After you land, be sure to spend some time shaking off your feathers and preening them back into place. Eat some spilled grain. Take a sip of water.

And if that doesn't fortify you, there's always a nice, frothy mug of pigeon milk.

FURTHER READING

Encyclopedia of Pigeon Breeds, Wendell M. Levi, Levi Publishing Co., 1965.

Levi was a powerhouse in the pigeon world, and this book is packed with photos and descriptions of many fascinating breeds.

Feral Pigeons, Richard F. Johnston and Marian Janiga, Oxford University Press, 1995.

The quintessential pigeon tome, this readable, authoritative book is beautifully illustrated.

The Genius of Birds, Jennifer Ackerman, Penguin Books, 2016.

Discover bird intelligence through fascinating studies and anecdotes.

The Global Pigeon, Colin Jerolmack, University of Chicago Press, 2013.

This is a riveting ethnography of people around the world whose lives intersect with pigeons.

Pigeons: The Fascinating Saga of the World's Most Revered and Reviled Bird, Andrew D. Blechman, Grove Press, 2007.

Enjoy a fun and thorough overview of pigeons and people— history, culture, and more.

Rock Pigeon (Columba livia), version 1.0, **Peter E. Lowther and Richard F. Johnston, in** *Birds of the World* **(S. M. Billerman, Editor), Cornell Lab of Ornithology, accessed in 2020.**

Peruse this excellent entry in Cornell's comprehensive *Birds of the World*. Then, do yourself a favor and subscribe to the whole thing!

Superdove: How the Pigeon Took Manhattan . . . And the World, Courtney Humphries, Smithsonian Books, 2008.

Treat yourself to an enjoyable read that explains how humans turned pigeons into the ideal urban species.

Unnatural Selection, Katrina van Grouw, Princeton University Press, 2018.

Released to celebrate the 150th anniversary of Darwin's *The Variation of Animals and Plants under Domestication,* this lavishly illustrated book blends Darwin's ideas with recent thought about evolution and the development of domestic animal breeds.

Victoria: The Biography of a Pigeon, Alice Renton, Ivy Books, 1988.

Grab a box of tissues and dive into this sweet, heartbreaking tale of a rescued pigeon who became part of the family.

SELECTED REFERENCES

36 Randa Kakish, "Evidence for Dove Breeding in the Iron Age: A Newly Discovered Dovecote at 'Ain al-Baida/'Amman," *Jordan Journal for History and Archaeology* 6, No 3 (January 2012).

63–64 Tzu-Ruei Yang and P. Martin Sander, "The Origin of the Bird's Beak: New Insights from Dinosaur Incubation Periods," *Royal Society Biology Letters* 14, No 5 (May 2018), doi.org/10.1098/rsbl.2018.0090.

72 Sarah E. Bush, Scott M. Villa, Juan C. Altuna, Kevin P. Johnson, Michael D. Shapiro, and Dale H. Clayton, "Host defense triggers rapid adaptive radiation in experimentally evolving parasites," *Evolution Letters* 3, No 2 (March 2019), doi.org/10.1002/evl3.104.

85 Shigeru Watanabe, Junko Sakamoto, and Masumi Wakita, "Pigeons' Discrimination of Paintings by Monet and Picasso," *Journal of the Experimental Analysis of Behavior* 63, No 2 (March 1995), doi.org/10.1901/jeab.1995.63-165.

85 Richard M. Levenson, Elizabeth A. Krupinski, Victor M. Navarro, and Edward A. Wasserman, "Pigeons (*Columba livia*) as Trainable Observers of Pathology and Radiology Breast Cancer Images," *PLoS ONE* 10, No 11 (November 2015), doi.org/10.1371/journal.pone.0141357.

85 Victor M. Navarro, Edward A. Wasserman, and Piotr Slomka, "Taking Pigeons to Heart: Birds Proficiently Diagnose Human

Cardiac Disease," *Learning & Behavior* 48, No 1 (March 2020), doi.org/10.3758/s13420-020-00410-z.

85 Robert G. Cook, Deborah G. Levison, Sarah R. Gillett, and Aaron P. Blaisdell, "Capacity and Limits of Associative Memory in Pigeons," *Psychonomic Bulletin & Review* 12, No 2 (April 2005), doi.org/10.3758/bf03196384.

85 Muhammad A. J. Qadri and Robert G. Cook, "Pigeons and Humans Use Action and Pose Information to Categorize Complex Human Behaviors," *Vision Research* 131 (February 2017), doi.org/10.1016/j.visres.2016.09.011.

85 Damian Scarf, Harlene Hayne, and Michael Colombo, "Pigeons on Par with Primates in Numerical Competence," *Science* 334, No 6063 (December 2011), doi.org/10.1126/science.1213357.

85 Damian Scarf, Karoline Boy, Anelisie Uber Reinert, Jack Devine, Onur Güntürkün, and Michael Colombo, "Orthographic Processing in Pigeons (*Columba livia*)," *Proceedings of the National Academy of Sciences of the United States of America* 113, No 40 (October 2016), doi.org/10.1073/pnas.1607870113.

94 Eric T. Domyan, Zev Kronenberg, Carlos R. Infante, Anna I. Vickrey, Sydney A. Stringham, Rebecca Bruders, Michael W. Guernsey, Sungdae Park, Jason Payne, Robert B. Beckstead, Gabrielle Kardon, Douglas B. Menke, Mark Yandell, and Michael D. Shapiro, "Molecular Shifts in Limb Identity Underlie

Development of Feathered Feet in Two Domestic Avian Species," *eLife* 5:e12115 (March 2016), doi.org/10.7554/eLife.12115.

106 Daniel Haag-Wackernagel, Philipp Heeb, and Andreas Leiss, "Phenotype-dependent Selection of Juvenile Urban Feral Pigeons *Columba livia*," *Bird Study* 53, No 2 (2006), doi.org/10.1080/00063650609461429.

107 Elizabeth Carlen and Jason Munshi-South, "Widespread Genetic Connectivity of Feral Pigeons Across the Northeastern Megacity," *Evolutionary Applications* 14, No 1 (January 2021), doi.org/10.1111/eva.12972.

131–132 Robert L. Niese and Bret W. Tobalske, "Specialized Primary Feathers Produce Tonal Sounds During Flight in Rock Pigeons (*Columba livia*)," *Journal of Experimental Biology* 219, No 14 (July 2016), doi.org/10.1242/jeb.131649.

132 Mae Hingee and Robert D. Magrath, "Flights of Fear: A Mechanical Wing Whistle Sounds the Alarm in a Flocking Bird," *Proceedings of the Royal Society B* 276, No 1676 (December 2009), doi.org/10.1098/rspb.2009.1110.

137 Ryan K. Tisdale, John A. Lesku, Gabriel J. L. Beckers, Alexei L. Vyssotski, and Niels C. Rattenborg, "The Low-Down on Sleeping Down Low: Pigeons Shift to Lighter Forms of Sleep When Sleeping Near the Ground," *Journal of Experimental Biology* 221 (October 2018), doi.org/10.1242/jeb.182634.

139 Dolores Martinez-Gonzalez, John A. Lesku, and Niels C. Rattenborg, "Increased EEG Spectral Power Density During Sleep Following Short-Term Sleep Deprivation in Pigeons

(Columba livia): Evidence for Avian Sleep Homeostasis," *Journal of Sleep Research* 17, No 2 (June 2008), doi.org/10.1111/j.1365-2869.2008.00636.x.

140 Nicholas M. A. Crouch, Vincent M. Lynch, and Julia A. Clarke, "A Re-evaluation of the Chemical Composition of Avian Urinary Excreta," *Journal of Ornithology* 161 (2020), doi.org/10.1007/s10336-019-01692-5.

158 Isobel Watts, Máté Nagy, Theresa Burt de Perera, and Dora Biro, "Misinformed Leaders Lose Influence Over Pigeon Flocks," *Royal Society Biology Letters* 12, No 9 (September 2016), doi.org/10.1098/rsbl.2016.0544.

186–187 Daniel Haag-Wackernagel and Holger Moch, "Health Hazards Posed by Feral Pigeons," *Journal of Infection* 48, No 4 (May 2004), doi.org/10.1016/j.jinf.2003.11.001.

193 Fayme Cai and Rebecca M. Calisi, "Seasons and Neighborhoods of High Lead Toxicity in New York City: The Feral Pigeon as a Bioindicator," *Chemosphere* 161 (October 2016), doi.org/10.1016/j.chemosphere.2016.07.002.

214 Elaina M. Tuttle, Alan O. Bergland, Marisa L. Korody, Michael S. Brewer, Daniel J. Newhouse, Patrick Minx, Maria Stager, Adam Betuel, Zachary A. Cheviron, Wesley C. Warren, Rusty A. Gonser, and Christopher N. Balakrishnan, "Divergence and Functional Degradation of a Sex Chromosome-like Supergene," *Current Biology* 26, No 3 (February 2016), doi.org/10.1016/j.cub.2015.11.069.

ACKNOWLEDGMENTS

Thank you to my thoughtful and persistent aunt, archaeologist and Egypt expert Mary McKercher, and to her colleague Dr. Jacobus van Dijk, for helping me learn about very early pigeon keeping. Thanks also to Professor Niek Veldhuis for elucidating the Mesopotamian angle. I'm deeply grateful to Katrina and Hein van Grouw for their many, many helpful emails about pigeon keeping and genetics. Genius researcher Elizabeth Carlen read an early version of this manuscript and sent me pictures of crested and feather-legged ferals. She also connected me with Richard F. Johnston and Marian Janiga's book *Feral Pigeons*, which is remarkable, thorough, and astonishing. Brian Rusnica, raptor expert, provided critical hawk info. My editor Danny Cooper was so thoughtful, funny, and patient throughout this project. Dr. Diane Kelly fact-checked this book and is also just the most fun person to talk to about animal genitalia in the history of the planet. The inimitable linguist Gretchen McCulloch was my pun consultant, so blame her for everything. Cynthia Tafoya-Stone provided great translation help. The whole team at Workman is the best darn flock in the world. To my agent, Seth Fishman, you are the wind beneath my wings. Thanks also to my sweetheart, always, always.

ABOUT THE AUTHOR

Rosemary Mosco is a science communicator, acclaimed cartoonist, and bestselling author. She is also a speaker on all things bird, and the creator of the webcomic *Bird and Moon*.